Conscious Love

Conscious Love

Enlightened Relationships and Soulful Sex

---

11 Love Experts Reveal Their Secrets

Christine Dunn, Dr. Elena Estanol
Kristina Shumilova. Joni Young
Deborah Morehead, Deborah Nielsen
Dr. Sky Blossoms, Lana Baumgartner
Christopher Menné, Lucia Nicola Evans

Featuring Alain Torres

BlissLife Press
San Diego

Published by BlissLife Press.

BlissLife Press
San Diego, CA
BlissLifePress.com

For ordering information or special discounts for bulk purchases, please contact BlissLife Press at BlissLifePress.com

First Edition

ISBN 978-0-9977392-0-6

Library of Congress Control Number: 2016945894

Cover design by BlissLife Press Team - Nan Akasha, Donna Sudiacal-San Pascual & Donna Arrogante

Book design by BlissLife Press Team - Christopher Sherrod

We LOVE Trees! For every book published at BlissLife Press we plant one hundred or more Trees. We support Trees for the Future, planting Tree farms that produce food, shade, clean air and a sustainable income.

Manufactured in the United States of America
10 9 8 7 6 5 4 3 2 1

Above All Is Love

Thank you for purchasing this BlissLife Press Book

Join our mailing list and get updates on new releases, deals, bonus content and other great books from BlissLife Press.

BlissLifePress.com

CONTENTS

Publishers Foreword

I believe that "Above All Is Love". I'm a lover, not a fighter. I've always been kind of quiet, but my all my adult life women would just come up and ask me out, so I had several relationships over the years. Yet, I was never willing to settle and to date just anyone, so I spent many years alone.

I waited, a long time. I am not sure what I was waiting for. A friend finally told me to just go on a lot of dates, a common technique now. Get a lot of practice and then you will find someone. It didn't appeal to me. So I continued to wait and work on my businesses. I went to a lot of meet-ups, but where I lived, few people went to those. I got a bit depressed as I thought I had to be perfect and super successful before I'd find anyone. In the end it was worth it. I met my Soulmate and I finally understood why people wanted to get married and stay together forever.

To be honest, I didn't really think about things like Soulmates back then. I was exploring spiritual growth, going to Abraham-Hicks meetings (back then they lived in the same town and were nowhere near as famous). Feeling energy and all that was totally new to me. So when I met my soulmate I didn't know it. I sat right next to her at a real estate investment meeting.

She was a successful real estate investor and was the speaker for this event. My dad and I were getting into investing and went to find out about pre-construction investing. After the talk ended, we stayed for a few hours chatting, we had a lot of things in common, especially business.

A couple of days later I called her, thinking it would be interesting to meet for lunch, purely business mind you. I had a friend doing real estate development in Costa Rica, and I thought she might be interested. All three of us (yes my dad came along) had discovered many topics we had in common, one being international investments.

Over the next couple of months, we all met every two weeks for lunch, and continued to discuss real estate investing. Other topics we had in common, began to come up, like travel, spirituality and prosperity consciousness. She had a women's real estate investing meeting and invited me to do my prosperity consciousness talk. After the meeting, we stood by her car for three hours talking, and even though I really enjoyed her, I still didn't think of her romantically.

Looking back now, it is interesting to see all the little things that began to build up to tell me "she is the one!". It was like a law of attraction movie! We would run into each other around town in random ways. I know now, that was destiny, but at the time I was still kind of down, and didn't think of dating anyone, even her.

All that changed one night, when we attended a dinner with Dr. Joe Vitale and Dr. Len. Joe brought over the Hawaiian shaman, Dr. Ihaleakala Hew Len, who healed a whole ward of criminally insane patients without ever seeing them. They eventually wrote a book called "Zero Limits" about the healing tradition of Ho'oponopono. She said something that caught by attention, and I looked at her... slowly it dawned on me... she's dateable!? Instantly my awareness shifted and I realized I wanted to date her. I came alive, an energy I had not felt in years coursed through my body, I looked at her and said "I'm interested, now what?"

It's now over 10 years later and I'm happier and more in love everyday. I fell deep in love fast, telling her I loved her within the first two months. I was so aware, she is the one, that I quickly had no interest in either of us dating anyone else. I asked her one day, "do you believe in Soulmates?" (she had decades of spiritual study and teaching). I knew inside me, that is what this was, I had found my Soul's match, and I was ready to go all in.

Conscious love is a lifestyle for me, not a catch phrase. I focus daily on being very conscious in my love relationship and attentive to my lover. It has paid off, with 10 years of true love and happiness. I feel more in love each day, and it still surprises me. I am very passionate about love. I believe that most couples do not spend enough time together, and there is not a lot of conscious thought and care put into relationships. I am grateful every day, and I tell her how I feel and express my love daily. Love relationships are precious, and I am committed to be conscious and caring in mine.

I feel sad about how unfulfilling, and unconscious most relationships are. How little caring attention is given to growing together as a couple and respecting each other as individuals. I see so many men who are confused when their wife leaves, after years of thinking they are doing the right thing. I have friends who worked all the time and made money, bought a house... only to discover what she really wanted was his loving attention and time. There are too many women feeling unseen, untouched and unfulfilled.

Higher consciousness in love, marriage, and partnerships of all kinds is overdue, and can solve a deep emptiness in most people. An enlightened relationship is about respect, and being fully present and aware of your partner's needs. It is natural, but society has given love relationships a framework that was more practical, and not enough emphasis on the deeper connection.

We are seeing changes and shifts in the world today towards gender fluidity, gay marriage and tolerance of couples who do not want to have children. The shift to more conscious thought is giving couples more choices and more acceptance in the realm of love. I am optimistic of what is coming, and I want to be leading this movement, hence the genesis of this book.

This book was born when I attended an event and met Alain Torres. We had a fascinating conversation about conscious love and what that meant. A couple of weeks later I'm sitting in my office thinking of how my publishing company can change the world. Alain texts me and -boom! - instantly I get this idea for a book "Conscious Love". I got a vision for a great book about conscious love, a topic I thought wasn't talked about enough.

I didn't just get inspired by Alain because of his "Power Couples Project", or even for his go for it attitude, friendly heart and connections. It was how he lived his love life. Consciously. Like Alain I'm totally in love and live the principles of conscious love daily. I wanted to get together other conscious love experts and start a discussion on what conscious love is and how to live it.

My partner in life and in our publishing house, BlissLife Press, Nan Akasha joined the project and we had a fantastic time getting all these leading experts into the book and co-creating it together. Our intention is that you get a vivid picture and a deeper understanding for what a conscious love relationship is and tools to help you live it. We wanted to bring together many perspectives and aspects of love relationships. You will resonate with some and not others. You will also be able to come back to this book at different times in your life, depending on what is happening, and find guidance.

Whether you are longing for love, or in a challenging relationship this book has answers for you. If you are hurt and afraid to love again, you will find ways to heal the past and love yourself. If you want to stop the same pattern repeating, and know how to turn conflict into connection, the path is here. From sensual connection through food, sacred sex or seeing how your love life and your money situation are all related, it's here.

Enjoy.

Christopher Sherrod
San Diego, CA
April 2016

Introduction

What is conscious love and why seek a new paradigm that
creates enlightened relationships and soulful sex?

Nan Akasha

The current paradigm of love relationships isn't working. Studies show sixty percent of people are unhappy in their relationships and marriages. Outdated systems for dating, relating and love are ready for a major redesign. It may sound odd, but this makes me happy. It's a great turning point on the planet, this 'upgrade' is well overdue. It's not enough anymore to play small, and settle for so much less than you were designed for. Consciousness is raising on the planet. Desire for a new kind conscious love relationship and a deeper, soulful sex life is growing.

This book is your invitation to break free from old patterns and repetitive relationships. Embrace a new way of being in love. A new way of being in relationship with yourself, and your partner, and the world.
We invite you to open your heart to love, and find a new connection that feeds your heart, Soul, body and mind. Let go of frustrations around lost love, hurtful breakups, or doubts you will ever find the "one". Rejoice in your dissatisfaction with current or past love experiences. The feeling you don't know how to make relationships work, is a calling to seek a new paradigm. It's an opportunity to answer the call for something more.

What if the love that didn't work for you in the past was actually just the training ground for the conscious love you are ready for? Would you be able to bless it, thank it, let it go and make way for the new? We have gathered 11 love experts to guide you. Use these new paths, perspectives and tools to take your love life from condemned to conscious. They will open you to a love that transcends your fears. Dissolve your blocks and open doors to new, delicious possibilities.

The system and paradigms around intimate relationships are changing. We are at a point in history where massive changes in consciousness are challenging our visions of what is possible in relationships. Men and women are unsatisfied with themselves, with each other and with what they create together, and often unhappy as well.

It is time for new paradigm for love. These soul-based experts in conscious relationships are leading the conversation.

I spent over 23 years in a lackluster marriage. I was in love, and my wedding day was one of my most happy at that point. But, it faded fast and the duties of life kept coming and I was being the "good girl". I kept moving forward, doing my best and thinking it would all get better again. I blamed myself, and kept trying to figure out what was wrong with me. Then I threw myself into my work, then my kids, then...

Our communication sucked and eventually the heaviness I carried everyday became normal. Even though I felt alone, guilty and like a failure, I kept up facades. We functioned like efficient roommates, taking care of house, kids and daily chores. I loved my house, but I hated being in my house, the energy was so oppressive. Anger, and resentment hung in the air. Even though we rarely argued, it felt like he was throwing daggers at me from his solar plexus as I crossed the room.

I gained more weight to protect myself, and probably to 'punish' myself as well. I fell into believing there was no way back to love, and that a hot sex life was a thing of the past and gone forever. There was nothing conscious about this love, it was judgmental, lonely and highly conditional. This relationship was not enlightened. Instead of soulful sex, it made me sick to my stomach, so I avoided it in many creative ways.

When I finally awakened to the realization I had to leave, I had manifested major health issues. I felt like I wanted to jump on a plane and run far away, and my whole body itched and my skin crawled. Over the next 3 and a half years my life and everything I had spent decades creating, fell apart. I ended up bankrupt and wondering where to live and how to feed my kids. To escape the unconscious love, I was willing to 'chew off my own paw' to get out.

What happened from this deconstruction was painful and magical, horrific and healing. One thing for sure, it made me committed to finding a higher love, and not settle for anything less. I was happy to be free, even though the freedom came at such a high price.

Six months into my divorce, my Soulmate appeared. I could feel him for two months before I met him in person, in my energy field, in my body and Soul. I kept guessing who it might be, while being annoyed because I was NOT looking for love. In fact I was trying to get out of one relationship, and did not want anyone else right now. I tried to "give" him to a friend, thinking he was such a great guy, but not me, not now. I even had visions of traveling the world and having a lover in each "port"...

When I surrendered my plan and pain to Source, I followed the advice of my wise business coach. He said "Play full out or get out now. Otherwise you will always wonder, and never know what it could have been".
That was powerful and wise guidance, and opened a door to conscious love for me. I made a commitment to only do what I truly desired and to

express myself authentically. I decided to only and always come from unconditional love. I used the "always assume the best" attitude toward him, and honored myself and my feelings. I paid close attention to any feelings or reactions that were echoes from the old relationship. Knowing these were not serving the highest purpose of love. I was willing to commit to conscious communication. To be honest and direct yet loving and kind, even when it scared me.

My reward was a conscious love relationship that feeds my Soul, mind, purpose, happiness and body. I never knew this kind of enlightened co-creative, respectful and uplifting relationship existed. I continue to be amazed, as it grows deeper and stronger daily, over ten years later. I had no awareness people woke up happy and loving, were loving and kind and loved you for who you were, not what they wanted you to be. I didn't know I could be accepted and loved and fulfilled, instead of being told "I was too much work" and I needed too much attention.

My whole life until we met, I never felt fully seen, and safe and accepted. I never felt solid in any relationship, or "filled up", because it was so conditional. I knew deep within, I was not loved as me, I was loved if I behaved properly. I was tolerated or possessed. I realize now, the reason I needed to hear I was loved over and over from my parents or my husband. It was because it was empty, like filling a hungry tummy with water, it didn't feed me or stick with me.

My Soulmate is Chris, my partner in life and business. He is my co-founder in BlissLife Press. Together we get to fulfill our life missions in business while living life in a conscious loving way. Sex was not over for me and isn't for you either. I found it was not me, it was the low vibration energy of the relationship.

Now my life with Chris is so fulfilling, it is hard to remember the past. Sensual, soulful, sacred sex. Kind, fun, loving friendship. Purposeful, fulfilling, conscious co-creative work (business). And a partner that allows me to be me, giving me safe space to be my full and true self. A conscious love relationship is possible, no matter how long you have waited or how many times you have had to move on.

What paradigm would you choose?

How would your life change if your dried-up old, non-existent sex life was suddenly wild, wet and rejuvenated again? There's no reason to think it is over, turn on soulful sex and find a new sacred connection to your partner in the pages of this book.

What if the cure to depression was as simple as passionate love-making? Imagine healing and renewing that deep connection and place of peace in your lovers arms.

What if the way to connection was through conflict? Our conscious tools flip that switch so you can see the opportunity, and love freely again.

What if moving on from love that didn't work out wasn't a painful, lonely, long dragged out process, but instead you had tools to open your heart to love and create a new love, based in authentic relating? You have those tools in your hands, use them!

There is always a solution, and here you can discover how to be YOU no matter what happened in the past. Come with us and uncover the truth; that conscious love is kind, patient, and trusting and you can learn to navigate pain as a map to your greatest joy. Enter this journey and enlighten your heart as well as your relationships.

Preface

My first love relationship ended when my girlfriend broke up with me in front of the entire third grade class. I felt as though my heart was stomped into the ground until nothing was left.

I went into hiding. I didn't come out for a very, very long time.

In my late teens, I pondered if this dramatic experience was a major turning point in my life. I wasn't able to see the big picture yet, but it raised some major questions in my mind. These have fueled my quest for a deeper understanding of love, and not just any love, but conscious love. And what I have found in that quest is that our relationships, especially our romantic ones, are the key to discovering true fulfillment and understanding the meaning of life.

In college, I had my first epiphany. I noticed how people were constantly repeating patterns practically always playing out identical reactions from situation to situation. I was fascinated by how easy it was to see the patterns in others. Usually, there were major blind spots for people; they couldn't see what they were doing. The foundation of my passion for conscious love clearly began at a young age.

As my eye for patterns refined, I had a second epiphany. I realized I was also stuck in my own patterns... I was no different. I wasn't special. My first major commitment to myself was when I decided to be mindful and conscious of how I was showing up in my relationships. I would be conscious of my patterns, my mental and emotional blocks. I quickly made the next commitment of working through the lessons no matter what came up, to learn how to get out as quickly as possible from experiencing the same things over and over again.

I have been deeply committed to growth and personal development since I was dumped in 3rd grade and have spent over two decades training myself to be able to experience the world through a heightened awareness of the five senses. This is how my consciousness has risen. I was a tinkerer and looked to understand and become aware of all the things I did (or didn't do) and why. I would ask myself questions like, "Why was I sabotaging love?" "Why was the spark dying out?" then questions like, "Where did that thought or emotion come from?" and finally, "Do I want to play out this pattern?" My friends and those closest to me always wanted to know what I had to say on their relationship situation; they never passed up the opportunity to ask away. I knew I was meant to master this and lead others, so I decided to focus the majority of my energy into this special type of love, Conscious Love.

This type of love is more than just being aware, awake, and understanding of your patterns. It involves self-exploration to examine where the mind unconsciously places meaning in your experience of life, so you can then set yourself free from those habits and patterns. It's also about seeing that the universe leaves you clues and offers valuable learning lessons through which only you are uniquely meant to evolve. Some of these include; why we hesitate to ask that special someone out on a date, why relationships fall apart over and over again, or why we drag our feet to take the next step with that special someone.

My once volatile relationship dynamic inspired me to keep digging deeper. I was not willing to settle for anything less than feeling true love and working through all the patterns that were holding me back from experiencing the life I desired to create.

My wife and I both sought this, not just within our relationship, but within ourselves. I married a woman to whom I've given five rings. I'll reveal more of that story in my chapter. It's been a continually enlightening experience for which I am forever grateful.

When I hit rock bottom and was searching for answers, I scoured resources, the internet, friends and family I looked up to, and frankly everything I could get my hands on. Nothing offered me the practical wisdom and insight that I sought to address the deeper meanings of life—spiritually and esoterically. I wanted something that addressed these relationships, with ourselves and with our partner, from a loving, respectful, and empowering perspective. I found resources, but they were disjointed; none offered me the map I was looking to help me navigate all of love.

One day, Chris, a friend and co-founder of BlissLife Press publishing, reached out and explained his vision for a book on conscious, loving relationships. The book would tap into a broad spectrum of love and relationship coaches and experts, each with their unique perspectives and first hand experiences that would reveal exactly how to create, attract, and develop a conscious love relationship. He wanted the world to have a resource to handle any relationship situation, including being single, in a truly unconditionally loving way. We agreed the world is complex, and not easy for many to find their way through, let alone nurture a relationship free from drama, ego, and jealousy. We both got off the phone excited about creating a guide that shared real expert advice, from an enlightened perspective. These are practical tools to apply and mindsets to implement to get real life results.

I knew it aligned with my purpose in life, and I was beyond excited! I immediately started reaching out to my peers, the top experts in the field of love, romance, marriage, sex, soulmates, and more. They could definitely hear and feel my excitement when I shared the concept of the book. They realized the same vision that Chris and I saw, and recognized the impact this book would make on the world. Each of us would share our unique experience and expertise in a way that is more well-rounded collectively, rather than just sharing our message individually.

I remember talking with one of the authors who was ecstatic that the message would be part of a collective purpose, vision, and message to the world. The book wasn't just about sharing their personal message but about having conscious love experts come together not in competition but in cooperation. In this way we lead by example, sharing what is possible when people come together with a shared intent and desired outcome.

This book will bring you a new way of being with yourself and others, and a new way of embodying higher ideals of consciousness in love relationships. It will support you through challenging break-ups, exciting times of falling in love, and moments of self-doubt or conflict. All of the expert authors here have experienced the highs and lows of love and their personal journeys have been catalysts for seeking the path of enlightened relationships and soulful sex.

If you struggle with why you feel ripped apart when someone betrays your trust, or are full of anger or blame towards your partner, past, present or future, or when your security and fears feel threatened you will now have a practical, conscious guide to turn to. This is a place where you will find the tools and processes that don't just answer the question "why" but also help you to understand and choose to live a different outcome. No matter what, you can always choose love. This is especially true when all the sirens are going off in your head and your heart is on the fence. This is why this book is so important to the world.

I have been blessed to work with world-renowned clients around the globe, have published articles in online publications like The Good Men Project, and have been featured on The Boston Globe, ABC, NBC, FOX, CBS, and others. The creation of this book has been one of my most rewarding projects. It wasn't without its challenges, but I have to say, the importance of getting this book to you far outweighed the obstacles we faced in completing this project. We've gone through the tough lessons so you don't have to go through them and stay stuck in them. We walked the path before you so know that you're not alone and no matter what your current situation, we've got you. This book is truly a gift that will give you the knowing and confidence that you're heading in the right direction.

If you're reading this right now, there's a high probability you're into meditation, yoga, eating healthy foods, and learning how to be present. This book is for navigating love in an aware and conscious way. It is for the seeker looking to find and understand the deeper meaning of truth and also why things really happen. There's no such thing a coincidences so I congratulate you in having this book full of wisdom come across your path. As you'll come to find (if you haven't already), conscious love is one of the most incredible paths of personal and spiritual development.

This book describes many different pathways of Conscious Love, and I'm confident you will find the right ones for you and your journey. Recognize that your path is an ever-evolving one. I highly recommend you come back to this book and revisit its wisdom as you evolve. You will use many perspectives, some together, some at different times, so use it as your secret love weapon each step of the way. Not only will it inspire, ignite, and bring you clarity, but when you re-read it, you will get something new and its words will sink even deeper into your soul.

I'm so excited to share this book with you. This is the book I wish I had when I was struggling to find direction, understanding, and guidance in love. I invite you to open your mind, heart, and soul as you read this book and apply its wisdom. Allow this to be a doorway to the conscious love your heart calls for. It will help you turn conflict into peace, miscommunication into understanding, and disconnection into partnership, in an effortless and easy way.

"You can get your fire and edge back. I want you to know that you can find your misplaced spark. That the person who knocked your out of your orbit doesn't have to hold you back. And in the end, you can find love, achieve your life's purpose, and become the ultimate team."

-Alain Torres

Let's get started.

Alain Torres
May 2016
San Diego, CA

What is a conscious love relationship?

Conscious love is a higher vibration, it encompasses you, and the 'all' simultaneously. It's when you, your partner and the impact you make on the world around you, come into alignment with your deepest values, and highest purpose.

It's "above all is love". You focus on giving love - to you and your partner, while staying committed to your personal purpose, and allowing theirs. It's when you honor each of your growth paths while growing together.
Conscious love is when you never put yourself below anyone, and you lift your lover up to new heights. You express yourself fully, appreciate, enjoy and receive. It's when being together creates more expansion not restriction and it makes everything better. Your partnership becomes a journey of exploration and evolution, bringing deep satisfaction in your emotional, mental and physical body.

Welcome to the path of conscious love relationships. You are here because you are called to take your experience of romantic love to the next level. To express your feelings and desires with honesty. To stretch yourself and to allow your partner to do the same, even if it triggers you. True healing happens at the edge, and it's safe to go there now, when you apply the wisdom in this book.

Each author has prepared powerful gifts for you. They help you apply their wisdom and tools and to deepen your shifts, and enhance your experience. Be sure to get them here: http://blisslifepress.com/conscious-love/bonuses/

With deep gratitude, reverence and love, I thank these courageous leaders. They are willing to step up, be vulnerable and offer real solutions. They are like heroes of the past, willing to forge a new path. They will take you deeper into truth, help you let go of limits. They are here to take your hand and show you another way, all in the name of true love.

To your juicy, happy, exciting, intimate, delicious, sacred, orgasmic, compassionate, fulfilling, expansive and uplifting love relationships. Enjoy with abandon! Play full out!

Love,

Nan Akasha

The Power Couple's Guide to Becoming the Ultimate Team: Secrets to Authentic Power through the Domains of Work, Play, and Love

Alain Torres

"You can get your fire and edge back. I want you to know that you can find your misplaced spark.
That the person who knocked your out of your orbit doesn't have to hold you back. And in the end,
you can find love, achieve your life's purpose, and become the ultimate team."
Alain Torres

I raised my right arm and let it fly...

...the extravagant engagement ring I was going to give her later that month.

Just ten minutes before, I felt torn. I couldn't believe how much love I put into that relationship. It was crazy to think I did everything possible to make it work and it still didn't.

I was sitting in my car crying about how I felt I'd lost myself — I tried so hard to be the person she expected me to be in our relationship. I did everything I could to prove my love.

In this moment of anger and grief, I decided the only way to move forward was to go to the top of a cliff— to make everything feel better.

In my heart I knew she was the one, but I was in shock.

The vision of our future together, our family, us always being together... It all disappeared in the blink of an eye. It wasn't on the table anymore. I felt like my life was over.

Five rings and nearly a decade later, and now she's my wife. What can I say? I love a challenge!

I wasn't always part of a Power Couple.
Before I met my wife, Xochitl (sounds like So-chill), I felt I was just like any other guy. I was coaching high-end clients twice my age on dating advice— they'd fly out to work with me, paying a pretty penny to learn how to meet "the one."

The problem I had with all that power is that it came with a massive amount of responsibility. Being 100% confident, I could walk up to anyone and get their number in under 30 minutes, I regularly got dates with my perfect 10 woman, and I was coaching others to do the same.

Like most power players and strong-willed people, I thought all the issues in my relationships were because of them, not me. I thought there was nothing wrong with me. As a power player, I didn't think I'd have to do any extra work. I felt I deserved my queen; that I was entitled to her.

If I'd only known then what I know now!

My wake-up call happened at a salsa dancing club, sitting at a table with an incredibly beautiful, and intelligent woman having a good ol' time. As I was watching her lips, listening to her words, I could hear that little voice in my head jibber-jabbering, saying: "Oh my god! She's just like your ex!"

It was like I was watching an old movie. She was a carbon copy of my ex — different face, same go-getter personality.

> I was pissed.
> I felt bad for her.
> I realized it wasn't her, it was me.

I felt bad for all the women I'd given up on over the years because I thought they were the problem. I was always blaming them rather than accepting responsibility for my actions (or lack thereof). The realization hit me as if I'd been socked in the gut.

That day triggered something deep within me. It's the very key that has enabled me to become so effective with Power Couples. At the time, it had only been three months since we'd split ways—I was crushed. Three years down the drain.

From the moment I met my wife, she knocked my freakin' socks off. Have you ever met that person yourself?

We were inseparable, and wow it felt beyond good... She was the woman of my dreams, the complete package.

We traveled the world together, experiencing life for all of its beauty and magic... I was the pilot and she was the co-pilot on our adventure-seeking explorations. We experienced cultures and places we'd only dreamed of seeing with our own eyes. We were on top of the world; there was nothing we couldn't do together.

We were amazing together, the dynamic duo, the ultimate team, growing into our Power Couple potential. So maybe launching her very extravagant engagement ring off the edge of a cliff into the ocean with all my might wasn't the smartest idea. But that impulsive moment was my wake-up call. That hot-headed action showed me not only that I wanted her in my life again, but also revealed what I needed to do to win the love of my life back.

That's the day I discovered the person I actually resented was myself — for creating a massive imbalance in the Three Domains of Authentic Power.

The "new love buzz" only lasted as long as we didn't try to change each other.

Unfortunately, this just wasn't our reality. We started pushing each other's buttons.

Now, don't let the beard and deep voice fool you... I'm a lover, not a fighter. While I am a second degree black belt and can definitely lay the hammer down, I much rather support others into bettering themselves. She was my queen, and I did all the little extra things that would make her happy — at least that's what I told myself.

When she was unhappy, I made it a practice to step up and be an even better man — I honestly never worked so hard for any relationship.

And...

I'd forgotten the most important lesson during my ten years of coaching other power players. My mantra was to be the best version of myself — to rise to the challenge and close the gap of disconnection.

In order to be a POWER partner, you have to embody:
Precision: know exactly what to do and how
Optimism: plan and achieve the best future
Warrorlike: have a never give up attitude
Excitement: make things fun and playful again
Reliable: no matter what, you can be counted on

When your Power Dynamic is in balance between your Domains of Work, Play, and Love, everything is perfect and you're on the same page — I call this Authentic Power. This is an overview of the exact system I use for all my clients; it will enlighten and help you break through your relationship situation. It will also reveal how being all or nothing keeps love stuck, stagnant, and unable to flow. As you read the following pages, be sure to use the illustration in the diagram below to better understand how the domains interact with each other. Perhaps, you have the Domain of Work under control, but lack Love and Play. Or, you have the Domain of Love handled but are struggling with the Domain of Work. Whatever your situation, when you have one domain out of balance, they're all off. This chapter will reveal your imbalance and set you on track to create Authentic Power, so you can stop feeling held back, become the ultimate team, and thrive in your life's purpose.

The Power Couples Guide to Becoming the Ultimate Team: Secrets to Authentic Power through the Domains of Work, Play, and Love

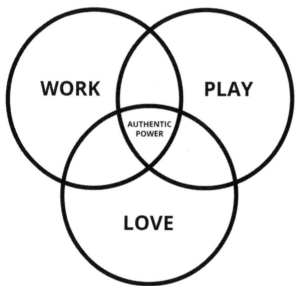

Authentic Power
*This diagram of Authentic Power will show you exactly where you're imbalanced in your Power Dynamic. Use it for reference as you read the following pages.

Know Yourself to Know Your Vision
Long before I met my wife, I remember standing in a classy lounge, when a stunning woman approached me. Without saying "Hi," she asked, "What do you do?". Clearly, my response wasn't what she wanted to hear, and supposedly saying I had a "very nice car" wasn't good enough as she left as quickly as she stormed in. Her world and my world were simply not a match. I commend her for being super clear on who she was looking for in a partner.

Many years later, I realized that what I was actually looking for in a woman wasn't what I was conveying through the questions I was asking on dates and how I was showing up in the world. It was no wonder I struggled for so long to find my match and often felt I wasn't being challenged and engaged in the way I wanted. My mind wanted one thing, but my heart wanted something different.

Because I've always been a high achiever with high standards, I wasn't willing to settle. The dilemma was, I didn't know who I truly was, and as a result, I didn't know who was to be my best match. I wasted a long time searching aimlessly, stumbling through my love life, not even knowing what I wanted or what it looked like. I helped one of my clients realize this exact thing. He was distracting himself from true love by just dating to date. He wasn't clear on his vision of love and as a result was only finding love on the level equal to what he committed to experiencing. This revealed his fear of love and also why his lack of clarity held him back from finding the love he searched so hard to find.

How many times have you gone on a date, really liked the person, but felt there was something missing? If you've experienced this, there's a high chance you don't know yourself well enough to recognize the person that complements you best.

Now, I recognize your nature is one of constant growth and achievement, but what do you truly stand for? What do you wish to create in the world, and why? Your answers to these questions may change over time, but the roots will almost always remain the same. When you start to understand more of who you are, you will know exactly who you want to spend the rest your life with. (For the complete list of questions, go to http://blisslifepress.com/conscious-love/bonuses/)

I remember speaking with a dear friend from Los Angeles, a quintessential playboy and working professional. He has everything in life except his Power Partner, and that's no accident. He set clear goals and has worked hard to achieve them. But relationships are a struggle, and he's yet to find a partner at his level. When I ask him what he wants, he replies, "I don't know." It's no coincidence that he's never happy about any of the women he dates, seeing he doesn't even know what lights his fire.

When we start to talk about the specifics, he gets uncomfortable. Whenever this happens with clients, it's usually very telling they've been pretty hurt in the past. You see, if you don't know who you are and where you come from, you'll be unconsciously playing out old habits, pre-recorded reactions, and emotions. When relationships don't go the way you want them to, it doesn't mean you're unlovable or unworthy of love: it simply means you've gotten yourself wrapped up in old patterns and continue to live them out.

It's my core belief that your relationships, especially with other Power Players, shed light on the "wounds" and "baggage" that you carry. When the conditions are right, they pop up, and there's no avoiding this. The magic happens when both you and your partner recognize this, and instead of pointing fingers, you support each other to heal what comes up. Talk about deep work! Getting to know yourself is the foundation for understanding how and why you relate to others the way you do — the good and the bad. With this knowing, you can be laser clear, like the woman in the lounge who knew what she was looking for when she approached me.

Your Authentic Power
This is what you're after. You want to have and experience the finest things in life, but you realize chasing these things won't complete you. Over the past decade of guiding world-renowned Power Couples and Power Players, there's been one major thread that everyone has shared.

Power.

I'm not talking about the evil take-over-the-world kind of power, but true inner power where you desire something because you choose to, not because you need to fill a hole. Of course you and I want to have it all, but true fulfillment comes from within. There's no substitute.

Looking back, I can see that hurt part of myself was craving inauthentic power, wanting to feel better and fill that gap. Being able to approach any woman I saw and get her to fall in love with me gave that temporary power. When that feeling wore off, I would move onto the next one, and then the next one, and so on... When I mastered that area of life, I realized I didn't feel any better than when I started off, but I did have a skillset that many others wanted but didn't have.

Just as I had, my clients sought to fill the void masked as true love. I quickly saw how humanity could do this to infinity in every single area of life. I wasn't going to fall for this trap, so I began my search for my Power Partner.

I didn't know what I was getting myself into, but looking back, I realize there's no way I would have achieved balance in the Three Domains of Authentic Power, on my own. My wife has shown me the gift of my buttons and has been instrumental for inspiring me to create this equilibrium. Without a doubt, it's been an incredible journey, one that continues to get better. When harmony is experienced in these Domains, Power Couples and Power Players can live from this place of true Authentic Power. There's nothing you can't do when you're there.

On the following pages, you'll see an overview of the domains. See which two you lead with. Trust your gut and listen to your intuition.

The First Domain of Authentic Power: Work
The Domain of Work is masculine. It is more of the actual doing in the world and creating things outside of you. It's usually the things that are more tangible, the achievements you can see with your eyes and sometimes feel with your fingers. The reason you work so hard in this domain is because it allows you to support the lifestyle you choose and the purpose both you and your loved ones wish to live out. Your strong work ethic provides the potential to play and have adventures in ways that most people can't.

The alarm went off every morning at 4:30, and off we went to the family business in Burbank, California. Before my dad was 20, he owned his first Porsche. Now he is globally recognized in the Porsche industry.

I can honestly say that we practically lived at his work building. We had a kitchen, a living room, and I even had a futon so I could take power naps when I got home from high school golf practice. My dad worked his tail off every day until at least 7 or 8 o'clock.

Without a doubt my upbringing definitely shaped how I showed up to my relationship with my wife. I thought it would make things easy, but boy was I wrong. In the beginning it created a massive divide. While I thought it was a total asset to have a strong work ethic in the relationship, it actually drove us further apart. All my time was focused on work and frankly I didn't stop. It started to take its toll on us and especially me. What do you think I did to try to create balance? That's right, I worked even harder and this created an even bigger gap. This ended up backfiring into a massive breakup, but I guess being a stubborn person, I had to learn the hard way.

The bottom line; I don't want you to learn the hard way if you don't have to. Check in with yourself, is the majority of your time and energy focused on your work life? If so, is this how you relate, showing and sharing your love and care from working your butt off? Whatever your answer, it's not a bad thing; it's just your truth right now. Be honest with yourself, become more aware, and adjust from here. It's not about actually working harder to create balance; it's about creating balance inside you. When you do this, you show up completely differently to your relationship: more present and more in alignment.

One of the hardest things I see my clients go through when they primarily come from the Domain of Work is they are so focused on results and timelines. I'll talk more about this in The Third Domain of Authentic Power: Love, but in short, love is illogical and spherical. What I mean by that is, it's not linear and always predictable. So if it is difficult to allow yourself to let go and flow, the questions I ask you are: When is the last time you surrendered to a particular outcome? And, what comes up for you when you ask yourself the question? What are your doubts, concerns, or limiting beliefs?

I remember asking my dad why he'd always worked so hard and why it never seemed like he took any breaks. His response was, "I'm doing this because I want to provide a good life for you and your mom, and I want to give you the best opportunities possible. If I stop, the money stops."

As with my dad, this is your ultimate sacrifice and the greatest thing you can give. It's your way of showing your love and care, your self-expression.

If this is you, make sure that you're actually taking care of yourself. I can't tell you how many times I see someone with this focus taking care of everyone else but themselves. What happens if something happens to you? I know you don't want to hear it, but take care of yourself and while you're at it, make time to do things with your loved ones, adventures, trips, or vacations so you can unplug, reset, and gain a fresh perspective on life. Not only will you benefit, but they will love you for it.

Being a Power Player, there's a high chance you lead with this domain. But just because you have it under control doesn't mean it's in balance with the Second and Third Domains of Authentic Power. Remember, you're loved ones don't just want what you bring to the table, but more importantly they want to spend quality time and experience life with you. The most important thing I want you to get out of this section and the others is to gain clarity on where you are at right now. Be honest with yourself so you can go from there to create true balance, true authentic power. If you can't be honest where you are with yourself then maybe you want to stay stuck. I sure hope not.

The Second Domain of Authentic Power: Play
The Domain of Play is the glue that brings everything together. It includes things that are fun and adventurous, especially things that are outside your comfort zone but are pleasurable to you. It comes in a whole variety of flavors. When you play, play all out and don't hold back. I find that people take love and relationships so seriously they forget to have fun and go crazy. Play acts as a master reset switch that gives you a fresh perspective on life — one that will undoubtedly unblock you when you feel stuck, stagnant, or overwhelmed in your dynamic.

I could feel the energy in the air. I slept through my alarm and this was the one day I couldn't afford to drop the ball. I could tell it was going to be one of those days.

I was in the kitchen making our morning green juice, and sensed I was out of sync with my wife. I could tell she was off and was spiraling out of control in some mental process. I said, "What's going on? What's wrong?" She then proceeded to unload everything that was wrong with how her family was handling a particular situation and how she thought they were making a huge mistake. All I could do was shut up, be quiet, and listen.

After she finished, I comforted her, but this wasn't enough to shake her out of her funk.

After things cooled down, I said with excitement, "I know! Let's go for a walk to the park with Uni (our Labradoodle) and then go to the beach after! We'll even pick up a pizza from Whole Foods!"

I can only imagine how the day would have continued for her if I hadn't dropped everything to go play. The truth is, I needed it too. And that's exactly what we did... we played and we played hard.

Fortunately, I was able to change the flow of my typical day to address what needed my attention most. The play element was a total game changer. It didn't need to be a trip to the Bahamas, all that was needed was a little break up of pattern. This is no different for you. My guess is you also have the fortune of being able to ebb and flow with your schedule, and if you don't, that's okay, just realize how important play time can be. It really brings renewed energy to you and your loved ones, so please schedule play into your daily life!

For Xochitl and me, travel is a huge vehicle to completely unplug and play. We frequently take time to travel abroad, go camping and hiking, and go on cross country road trips. There have been times we'd rough it on a couch, other times, we'd stay in a private hacienda in Mexico, and another time, we stayed in an eco-lodge on the Amazon River bank. The biggest distinction I would like to make is it's always about consciously deciding what you want to experience together. Even if you're planning play time for yourself, decide to do something that really feeds and nourishes your soul; something that really makes you happy and that has you smiling from ear to ear. This isn't something hard to do; you just have to make time for it and do it. Trust me, it'll make a massive difference.

So what are some of the things you can think of right now that you can decide to do to play? List them out, and then schedule them into your life. I strongly suggest scheduling some play time for yourself as well. This is equally important as it helps you mentally and emotionally to process things that are going on in your love life. I also highly recommend that you take your play time seriously and don't think about a single thing other than what you're doing. Use this time to reflect and also to detach from things that are on top of your mind. This takes you out of your patterns and sets you free to see all things from a new light. I'll leave you with this; think of children having fun and playing. Do you think they have a care in the world? No, they usually don't. Regain that innocence, even if it's just for 30 minutes. You'll notice a difference and so will everyone else. You'll be buzzing and everyone will find that highly attractive.

The Third Domain of Authentic Power: Love
The Domain of Love is feminine. It's really about the growth of learning how to unconditionally open your heart regardless of what happens in your

journey of love. Nobody ever said love was easy. It will inspire you to grow in ways you didn't know were possible. In your love life, it's all about you sharing this vulnerable, infinite part of you with that special someone. It's a continual dance where you also receive someone else's love; where you both journey into yourselves as you inspire trust and openness within one another to go even deeper.

This domain is about catering to your King or Queen. It's where you want to give them the world and show them how much they really mean to you. It's not just words, it's actions and the way you express yourself to them. In my ten years of experience, I believe you've uncovered true love within yourself when you love someone so much you're willing to put them before you. And when they also feel this way about you, you've met the Power Player that will complete your Power Couple.

You'll find yourself doing things you've never done before, things you never thought you'd do for anyone. You go above and beyond and will move mountains when needed. This is the person who will teach more about yourself than anyone before. In the domain of love, you'll find yourself having profound conversations, talking about your deepest secrets, visions, and ideas to make a difference in the world. The possibilities are endless as you feel so much more powerful with them by your side. At times they can push your buttons, but there's nobody else you'd rather be with.

As the weekend ended, I could tell Xochitl was beyond preoccupied when she left for work. The dishes in the kitchen sink were piled sky high and it looked as if a mini bomb went off on the countertop. You know the feeling of, "Where do I start?!" Well, we started the night before, cooking up a storm and playing in the kitchen together; the responsibility was left on my shoulders to tidy everything up.

I didn't stop when the kitchen was clean, I cleaned her entire place. The vision of her being overwhelmed was my motivation that fueled me. I did it because I cared. I did it because I wanted to show her my love. And to be honest, I did it with the expectation of being acknowledged and loved back. This was my number one mistake. If you're giving to get in your love life (yes, even dating), you will only set yourself up for frustration and heartbreak. This usually means that you lead with the domain of love and don't maintain a balance with the other domains of work and play.

If you're overpowering with love, are you loving just to love or are you protecting to prevent from losing love? Why? And if you're not experiencing the type of love you would like, what's holding you back from feeling that deeper level of love within yourself and with your partner? Why? After answering these questions, you will know exactly what's getting in the way of true love. Hint, balancing the other domains is the remedy. I want you to have this balance; it's epic and conscious love is everything that you've ever heard and more.

One of the biggest lessons I have learned through love is the art of giving just because you want to. When you do this, all of your inner stuff comes up. Self-worth, self-love, confidence, truthfully an infinite amount of emotions and thoughts. When you love unconditionally, and give just to give, it teaches you a lot about yourself. Even for my clients who have children, and find it easy with them, they still find it hard with their partner. Don't feel alien if this is you, just know that it's normal and you can work through it. Love will teach you the meaning of life and your own unique purpose. It is a lifelong teacher, hold to the vision of love — it will never lead you astray.

So now that you've read the overview of the Domains, which domain do you lead with and which comes in close second? Knowing this will show you the domain you're out of balance with. Go to http://blisslifepress.com/ conscious-love/bonuses/ to check out the video training to go deeper into the Three Domains of Authentic Power. This is the tip of the iceberg.

I'd Like to Introduce You to Your Power Partner
Like the conductor of a symphony, she would command the room making space for her mat when she was late. Where others came and left because they didn't see space, she came in and always made space. I couldn't help but notice the massive ripple effect of her presence when she entered the yoga room. My first thoughts were, "Who the hell does she think she is?" followed by, "I like her. Game on. I'm going to go talk to her." How irrational, right? In nearly a decade, I'm happy to report my wife has yet to disappoint. From the moment I met her, I knew deep down she was my match and she'd give me a run for my money.

Many people ask me, "How do I know I've met my Power Partner?" I always respond, "Trust me, you'll know it!" It's undeniable when you meet them, you just know they're going to push you in ways that no one else ever has. The interesting thing is, you'll even welcome it. The passion is off the charts — you just can't get enough of them, you're like one another's drug.

I had just moved back to Los Angeles, but there I was driving practically EVERY weekend back and forth from Los Angeles to San Diego — two hours each way — just to spend whatever time I could with her. This went on well over two years. Talk about commitment. Was the distance easy? No, definitely not.

A month into our relationship, we went to the Yucatan, Mexico. The things we did were impulsive and adventurous, like going into the jungle and climbing ancient Mayan pyramids, and visiting rural villages of native peoples. Then, two months later in Hawaii, we made some dangerous hikes, climbing to the bases of waterfalls we had no business attempting. Talk about living life on the edge! I felt so alive, yet also at times, so internally torn and terrified. She sent me to the moon and back, but when the honeymoon phase wore off, she also sent me plummeting back to the Earth. When the times were good they were beyond good, but when times were bad, they were beyond bad.

This relationship dynamic was unlike any I had ever been in before. My wife brought out my best and also my worst. In the beginning, she would blame and point every possible finger, making me wrong even when I knew in my heart I didn't mean it in the way she took it. How do you convince the person you love to see the situation from a different perspective, especially when they're just as stubborn and strong-willed as you?

What to Do When You Lock Horns
I'll explain exactly what you need to do in this situation. But first, I have to tell you that the difference between understanding what to do logically and the difference between completely embodying this knowledge is what separates Conscious Relationships from Enlightened Relationships. They're night and day. One understands the theories and the other is living a different relationship situation entirely.

The more I've done this work with highly successful movers and shakers of the world, the more I've realized there is no such thing as coincidences. It's like clockwork, you will practically always attract the person who will reveal your deepest "wounds." And this person offers you the one-way ticket to free yourself of your patterns once and for all. Even though it gets tough, it's a blessing in disguise, and you'll find your partner's "baggage" fits yours like a perfect puzzle piece. To avoid growing pains, you must know exactly how to heal what comes up on the fly.

When locking horns, don't pour fuel on a fire. Allow your partner to get it all out; clearly they need to process what they're saying. Don't take personally anything they're saying, especially when it's directed at you. And, don't defend yourself, even if you know you're right, as this will only escalate the situation. Easier said than done, right?

This is where your inner work comes in and really is the basis in how you move from Conscious Couple to Enlightened Power Couple. Standard communication skills won't work in these situations. Many other relationship experts will teach you all the best communication skills, saying they will solve all your communication breakdowns, but when a habitual reaction arises, this is something that needs to be addressed inwardly. Trust me: I've had to learn the hard way. We went to see counselors, psychologists, communication experts, hypnotists, psychics, palm readers, astrologists, did multiple past life regressions, and even went to see shamans. I know what works and what doesn't.

It was very hard seeking proper help. The vast majority didn't have any firsthand experience of what we were going through. Where they did, they weren't successful in working through their situation. Some referred to their textbooks, citing studies and journals and this didn't give us any confidence in their ability to guide us. I took bits and pieces of knowledge from each of them and was able to help us succeed. I found the secret that turned our whole relationship around. This same secret will ensure you don't give up and walk away from the love of your life.

One of the most important lessons I leave you with in this section is to take 100% responsibility for yourself. This includes your actions, your thoughts, your words, and your emotions, both conscious and unconscious. Blaming and projecting your "stuff" onto someone else is not taking ownership. Once you adopt this mindset, more than half the battle is over and you'll quickly move towards becoming the Power Couple you know is possible.

Bringing it All Together: Next Steps
At a high-end business event, I struck up a conversation with another Relationship Expert and Coach. She had this strong belief that if she moved to a far-off cave in a remote location, she could achieve enlightenment in the blink of an eye. This just isn't true. You see, if you're constantly tippy-toeing around life and your relationships, avoiding all the things that push your buttons, you're in a state of fear. If you only put yourself in situations where nothing triggers you, you're running from the true work that will set you free from your triggers and reactions. It's like going to the gym, and expecting to get stronger just by looking at all the equipment: it's just not possible. There's a reason they say, "no pain, no gain."

I know your Power Dynamic has become one of your greatest tests, so allow yourself to face your doubt, your worry, and your frustration head-on. Be decisive; give yourself the permission to work through everything that makes you think twice. This overview will give you the confidence to know there is a map to succeed even though you feel you're going in opposite directions from love. This is why reaching Authentic Power is so important. It allows you to stand in your power so you can stop tiptoeing around love.

My only wish for you, is that you set yourself up to win. One of the greatest lessons I've learned in life is to ask for help. The truth is, I wasn't always open for asking for help. I wanted to feel the gratification of figuring it all out on my own. Fortunately, I opened my mind and saw that getting assistance from someone who had walked the path before me was a massive benefit. I increased my chances of success, and also cut my learning curve significantly. This means less heartache, drama, and butting heads. I still pinch myself every day, knowing what my wife and I worked through to heal our chaotic dynamic. It was practically a miracle. Where millions of couples have failed, we figured it out. You too can have success in love and in your relationship. We're proof of it.

Are you ready to experience the love you always knew was possible? It's empowering to have a proven system to find love and be on the same team. It's time to stop searching; you've found the help you've been looking for. Today's the day you choose your relationship fate.

To get access to my three part video series— How to Stop the Power Struggle of Love and Start Feeling More Passion, Love, and Connection. Go to http://blisslifepress.com/conscious-love/bonuses/ now, to get immediate access to this training.

Making Sensual Love in the Kitchen

Lana Baumgartner

"The deepest pleasure emerges in the rapture of conscious love. Human life is a gift that can be ignited and savored in the expression of intimacy with your lover.
When you see into the eyes of your beloved, taste the sweetness of their soul, hear the palatability of their words, smell the aroma of their being, and feel them melting into yourself, the merging of two souls can serve as catalyst for the most authentic pleasure — yearning to be experienced."
Lana Baumgartner

Joe and I spent our first night together on the 24th floor of the Atlantic Palace in Atlantic City, New Jersey, in a bathtub, on MDMA (a synthetic psychoactive substance that induces a euphoric state of being). "Man's Eternal Quest" by Paramahansa Yogananda was the book I handed Joe, five minutes after we ingested the MDMA. Joe propped himself up against the window, with a backdrop of the Atlantic ocean glimmering under the light of the auspicious full moon. As he read, and engaged with the spiritual teachings of Yogananda, I reconnected with my five-year-old self. I filled the bathtub with the entire contents of four travel-sized shampoo bottles to create a massive mountain of bubbles. Ten minutes or so after sinking into the tub, as I watched the mound of bubbles ooze onto the floor, Joe burst through the door of the bathroom and professed, "I love you!"

I giggled and echoed, "I love you too! Get in the tub!"

As sensual as an MDMA experience can be, we ebulliently focused on unraveling the depths of our thoughts verbally and never engaged physically. We had just enough space to sit opposite each other, and maintain eye contact for a rather cosmic, philosophical, four hour conversation about saving the world and transforming our lives.

At twenty-two years old, my identity was wrapped up in anything deemed "yogic." Every ounce of my determination and ambition was laser focused on getting to a yoga teacher training in Mumbai, India that would begin in the fall of 2008. I had been practicing yoga, and fully immersed myself in what I thought of as a yogic lifestyle for a year prior to this, and was preaching to everyone I met. I was convinced that all problems could be solved by a dedicated yoga practice. Thus, I breathed, spoke, walked, read and most importantly ate, anything deemed "yogic." I was fanatical, simply put.

It might not be surprising that my relationship experience is rather unconventional. Actually, I hope it's not surprising at all, because we both know that there are no standard teachings, textbooks or courses in conscious relationships. Learning takes place through trial and error, and over time— through experience. There are hundreds, maybe thousands of books about how to create happy, stable relationships. I have to be completely honest. I can't preach about any shortcuts or hacks. Each partner brings their experience and wisdom to the table and it truly takes time and desire to co-create. What Joe and I brought to the table was a desire to learn and grow, together. When we finally decided commit to a relationship (find more of that story here: http://blisslifepress.com/conscious-love/bonuses/), we both had some learning to do. I can admit that I may have needed a bit more time to find my way than Joe. His mother had been in a happy, stable relationship with her lover for over twenty years. As for me, there were many beautiful, joyous moments during my childhood. However, these memories were not associated with conscious relationships.

I remember being in a convertible car somewhere in my hometown of Madison, Wisconsin. My mother was in the front passenger seat, and my father was driving. We were parked in a strip mall, in front of a florist shop. I don't remember the conversation that led up to the moment, but I do remember sitting in the back seat watching a clay pot fly out of the car and smash on the concrete sidewalk to our left. The noise of the clay shattering was followed by furious contention between my parents, and then my mother jumped out of the convertible in tears. I have quite a few more stories, much like this one. I recall them solely to serve as lessons in my own relationships. For many years it was painful to look back, but the only thing I can change is the cycle and I feel that it is my responsibility to do just that.

It's not helpful to judge my parents for what felt like chaos, rather seeing where they may have been coming from feels like a much more valuable approach. One of my most beloved teachers, Fred Weaver, III, M.D. teaches that we are only expressing our childhood wounds when in conflict with a lover. Did one parent disappear early on? Was one parent extremely stern, or hard to please? These challenges can play out for years, and often, into adulthood. I've been with Joe for nearly a decade now, and now that I have awareness of this concept, the truth has become blatant.

Fortunately, my father David, and mother Kathleen did teach me about love. They both taught me an abundance of ways to express love. I also learned exactly what didn't work in a relationship very early in life. Screaming, yelling, physical abuse, and threats never seemed to work to anyone's advantage. In the short time that my parents were together, I rarely witnessed extended periods of compassion, devotion or empathy (three key elements of a conscious relationship). It's funny how my memory works. I have a few photos of my chubby little body in between

Kathleen and David, all of us with big smiles and a warm glow. There was love, without a shadow of a doubt, but I know it was a challenge for my parents to maintain harmony without reprogramming what they had learned as children. My grandmothers on either side were both hopelessly devoted to marriages that lacked stability. One grandmother stayed in a physically and mentally abusive relationship, until my grandfather passed. The other grandmother stayed single until she departed from this physical world, after my grandfather left her.

It's challenging to determine what makes one individual respond to a stimulus in one way or another, but my history and experiences allowed me to choose persistence. From these early experiences, I decided that I must persist. My first long-term relationship lasted seven years, from the juvenile age of 15, until I finally realized that it wasn't working at 22. This volatile relationship was a constant struggle, and despite the young age, I can assume much of the responsibility for this seeming incompatibility. I left and returned multiple times over the seven years, and was always looking for something that I didn't believe was right in front of me. My confidence was rather non-existent, my trust could be lost an instant, and my commitment was inconsistent. I constantly questioned whether or not he loved me, if I could trust him, and caused myself years of tears and sleepless nights.

Before making a firm decision to move on from the destructive relationship, I consulted a mentor in my life, my uncle Jeffrey Kundert. He's a man who's turned his early struggles in life into success in almost every aspect of life. He reminded me that stable relationships require compromise. I interpreted that as selflessness (as opposed to selfishness). I was basically the opposite throughout the relationship. It was nearly impossible for me to put him first or even to comprehend what it felt like to be in his shoes. Jeff also firmly stated that "you'll never get 'better' you'll only get 'different.'" It took me a long time to understand what this meant, but today I can tell you that it's one of the best pieces of advice I've received. What I've come to understand is that we can change partners over and over, and instead of finding someone that's just perfect for us, or is the "one," we just end up with different challenges to work through. More importantly, we just keep finding ourselves, standing in front of ourselves. You leave your partner to find another, and there you are, again and again. In every relationship, there's work to do. When you find the "one," they aren't necessarily going to be everything you're looking for in a partner. It's more likely that they'll be the one who is willing to do "the work." They're the one who is going to look at all of the bullshit, and all of the baggage you leave in front of them (or sometimes hurl right at them), and ask how they can support you. They might not always respond with love in a tense situation, but they will always come around. They're open to the challenge, and ready to put the effort in, and move through. I have found this to be the "must" in our relationship. We must continually step up to the plate. What happens when the batter no longer steps up to the plate? The game is over. If one person is no longer willing to encounter a challenge, and move through, the relationship is over. Of course Mr. or Mrs. Right will have many of the sought-after characteristics, and this is important. The unwavering willingness to move through challenges, to grow and learn together is of the utmost importance. This willingness is what has allowed Joe and ME to reach nearly a decade of partnership. We're willing to do the work.

When I met Joe, our worlds collided, and I'll just offer the idiom, "all hell broke loose." With bubbles and emotions overflowing from that bathtub the night that Joe and I met, we poured our hearts out and contrived elaborate plans to change the world. We'd begin by starting a mass movement to hug president George Bush, and launch eco-commerce sites like "vbay," the vegan rival to ebay. I moved into Joe's home the following day, in May's Landing, New Jersey, after this sleepless night of world-saving in the bathtub. The plan was to be a roommate on the third floor of Joe's townhome from May 19, 2008 until I traveled to India, in September that same year. I would then embark upon my one to three year study, to become a yoga teacher and actualize my dream of teaching yoga to struggling children in Africa.

Within three days of moving in, I had become Joe's personal live-in health coach. I'd agreed in that bathtub to teach Joe everything I knew about health, in trade for my room in his house. I also had to help him keep the house clean (he likes to add to this part of the story that I must have forgotten that part of the deal). My mother had dedicated her life to becoming an herbalist and educating her clients about nutrition while I was in elementary school, and I'd come full circle as an employee at a Natural Foods Cooperative while in college. In high school, I took pride in drinking my minty green chlorophyll water, and writing articles for the school newspaper about the dangers high fructose corn syrup. I certainly did have a strong grasp on the basics, and I was eager to convert everyone who crossed my path into a food activist. Of course, this approach was a huge part of my "yogic" path (or so I thought). I was very satisfied exploring my identity as a self-proclaimed health guru, and years later, I've come to find that I was just scratching the surface when I met Joe that summer of 2008. He was just as eager to learn from me, as I was to teach him everything I knew. The dynamic was exceptional.

Joe asked me to clean out the kitchen and toss everything that I wouldn't eat. I adamantly crawled up on the counter (I'm only 5'1") , and stood on the countertop before each cabinet with an empty brown paper bag. Within a few hours, I'd completely cleared out the cabinets, refrigerator and freezer. We stood with our hands on our hips with a feeling of accomplishment for only a few minutes before we realized that we had nothing to eat for lunch. In South Jersey, there weren't many options for replenishing the kitchen. We drove almost an hour to Cherry Hill, toward Philadelphia to visit the nearest Whole Foods Market. We'd collected the basics about $1000 later, and from there the journey really began. Our relationship truly grew out of that little kitchen that Joe had renovated in his first home. We created beautiful memories together in that kitchen for three years. We reveled in sheer joy simply inviting friends over for a meal, or just to try one of our new creations. When we moved to California in 2011, with Joe's son, Joey, our love of food really expanded into a way of life. More and more friends and family would call asking for health advice; this not only translated into physical health, but health in every aspect branched from the idea of a love-filled kitchen. In the words of Joe's cheeky, wise Italian grandmother, "the kitchen is the cornerstone of a happy family."

Over the course of four years, Joe and I lived in New Jersey together; split after a few months and found each other just under one year later. The India trip did happen despite the deep bond that Joe and I had cultivated in just a few short months. I did take the yoga teacher training, but I didn't stay long. During one of the Sunday dinners, I sat at the kitchen table with four of Joe's cousins, his aunt, uncle and grandmother.

That same cheeky and incredibly comical grandmother leaned in and warned me, "You can't do that. You can't go to India. You'll regret it. Don't do it." Her voice rang in my head throughout the entire visit to India. I made my way back, to live with a friend, as Joe and I had separated only one week after I landed in Mumbai. I returned from India to my hometown of Madison, with a broken heart and hepatitis A. I hadn't completed the one year yoga teacher training. My dream was shattered.

When I recovered from hepatitis, I made my way to Southern California to move in with my friend from high school; Tera. The challenge of living in a new environment, still completely heartbroken, was too overwhelming, and I left in fewer than thirty days to move to Orlando with a Brazilian family. Secretly, I was praying that Joe, my prince charming, would rescue me in Florida, on his galloping horse, and profess his love, once again.

Joe had been visiting Florida every year, and I knew the chances reconnecting were much higher with my choice of relocation. It took what felt like a grueling eternity, but my plan worked. Joe took his annual trip to South Florida and we arranged a meeting. I was thirty pounds heavier than the day I boarded the flight to India, and in terms of health, a complete wreck. I woke up each morning in Orlando, wondering how I could find a way to make the day pass, and waiting to sit on the phone with Joe. I lost control of my emotions and became so depressed that my health was put on the backburner. Being depressed kept me from seeking out better financial opportunities, which kept me broke and unable to support myself. My eating habits were unintentional and incomplete, and I became severely drained and fatigued living on overcooked conventional produce, and white rice. When the day finally came; the day I'd been anticipating. The day where I'd reconnect with my beloved, I looked in the mirror in disbelief. I'd almost completely lost myself.

It was difficult to face him, but all of my concerns disappeared the instant that I met his eyes, in a tiny Cuban cafe in Miami Beach. I turned from the counter where I was buying a bottle of water to see Joe walking briskly toward me. It was the most emotional hug I've ever experienced.

Joe and I not only met in Florida, I flew back home with him, and stayed in what felt like a completely unfamiliar home for a week. I remember being awkward and uncomfortable. I was scared. I had missed him so much and I was scared to love because I knew it was temporary. We had only agreed on a friendly meeting to give our ears a break. After spending countless hours on the phone, it only made sense to see each other. We had spoken on the phone almost every day for the past six months. We attempted to avoid the subject of being together and focused on what was going on that day. Mostly, I'd just listen to Joe talk, and hang up wishing I'd listened to his grandmother's advice. I left South Jersey after our week-long friendly visit, and moved back to Wisconsin to rebuild my life.

The simplest option was to go back to what was familiar. I dived right into working countless hours as an exotic dancer to earn enough to rebuild my life. It took a few months of being home in Madison, finding my flow, until I finally felt like myself again. The self that I felt slip away that moment that Joe called me up in India, and said he didn't want to be my partner, was regained. Our brief meeting in Florida, and then traveling back to the home we lived in together, only made it more of a challenge to pull through. A month had passed since I moved back to Madison. I'd just earned enough dancing the week before to buy a new car, as I sold mine before leaving for India. I was on my way to pick up my younger sister a few hours north of Madison. Joe called, as he did almost every day, and asked where I was. I wasn't suspicious, as this was a usual question, but this time he sounded more demanding. I asked why, instead of answering his question. He said, "Well, I'm at your house." I felt my heart literally skip a beat, and almost lost control of the vehicle. "What do you mean, you're 'at my house?'" Joe said, "I'm outside of your door, on East Johnson." I just kept repeating that it couldn't be true. It was over an hour before I could make it back to my house, and ended up meeting Joe at a coffee shop on State Street in downtown Madison. My heart melted as he walked out the door and embraced me. I asked what he was doing and he looked into my eyes and said, "will you come back home with me?"

In the months that followed, we had to re-learn how to be with each other after. I felt that fear creep in from time to time; that fear that I first felt when I was visiting after we met in Florida. I wanted to make it work. I was ready to put the effort in. I knew that I wanted to be in partnership with Joe, or I wouldn't have been so lost and heartbroken for those eight months.

We were fortunate. It wasn't hard to build on what had become second nature. We just got right back in the kitchen where we had created most of our early cherished memories. We stepped up our game and ordered the local Community Supported Agriculture, or CSA. It was the most vibrant, organic, local produce, delivered right to our door (Jah's Creation, you'll always have a special place in our hearts). Did I mention that I was a horrible chef when Joe and I met? I honestly had no idea what I was doing in the kitchen, and following recipes made me want to pull my hair out. I learned through experimentation, and Joe was my most trusted food-critic. He'd try anything and always gave positive feedback first. In essence, he was—and is actually my greatest teacher. He taught me to keep going back to the chopping block (pun intended), and keep creating until I learned to master my craft. Love was my fuel. You are unstoppable when love is real.

The only thing I really felt confident doing in the kitchen was baking cookies. At five years old, my mother deemed me the official pourer of the brown sugar and vanilla. What I learned through watching my mother, was that after mixing the batter a hundred times, there's no need for a recipe. Joe and I still love cookies, but our intention is maintaining optimal health, which means more organic produce and fewer over-processed cookies. However, we did manage to devour large quantities of cookies in our early year together. The cookies are actually an integral part of the story. We eliminated refined sugar from our lives in late 2014, and it was a massive shift for both of us. Even though we didn't binge on boxes of Krispy Kreme donuts or slam a Coca-Cola for a midday pick-me-up, small amounts of the white stuff sneaked in through all of our "snacks." We weren't strangers to reading labels, but adding sugar to the list was shocking. Not because it's literally in everything, but because it's frequently disguised in the supposed "healthier" options. Joe was the first to make a firm decision. He watched a video that I sent him about the harmful effects of sugar on the human body, and vowed to give it up—that day; which I love about him. The humor lies in the fact that I never actually watched the entire video myself and it was a major catalyst in my life. Joe was telling a friend of ours how the video inspired him to make the shift, and looked to me to help explain the video. When he noticed my blank stare, he exclaimed, "you didn't even watch it, did you?" I bit my lip and looked away as if he wasn't asking me a question. I completely let him take the reins for us on this one. It took me a few months to join him, but when I did, it was one of those true cartoonesque lightbulb moments. What we eat really does affect our relationship in a profound way. This was yet another major decision that affirmed our shared, and simple understanding of the adage, "garbage in, garbage out" (borrowed from Joe's years as a tech geek). Giving up refined sugar was a clear decision to step up our game in a big way. Joe's biggest motivation was the thought of being controlled. The effect that sugar has on the brain is quite similar to cocaine or any other addictive substance. "Phening" for sugar is real, and Joe wasn't having it. We decided many years ago that we want full control of our biochemistry, and being addicted to any substance completely falls out of alignment with this desire. When research shows that cocaine and heroin are actually less addictive than cookies, logic wins.

The sugar shift was just one of the many evolutions in our relationship, and in the microcosm of our kitchen. I find it helpful to view the kitchen as an analogy, or microcosm, of the relationship, or macrocosm; which more literally translates to the entire universe. One thing that really stands out in my relationship with Joe is our roles as each other's teachers. We didn't formally assign these roles, but the intention of consciously interacting with one another resulted in this type of exchange. We trust that there's always something we can learn from one another. As I mentioned, Joe did in fact, ask me to teach him about nutrition, but the lessons that have proved to be most profound are frequently unspoken. Perhaps my attention to synchronicities is more of an awareness that Joe inspired, as opposed to a "lesson." Joe loves to point out, and to discuss, synchronicities. Basically, how this led to that, and how everything just aligned for it to all come together. I grew up around a lot of negativity and cynicism. Something I loved about Joe, the day we met, was his exceedingly optimistic perspective. I constantly strive to view the world in a similar way. The sensual kitchen and the concept of a "Sensual Foodist" was birthed through a synchronistic series of events.

On our flight back home from a networking marketing event for renewable energy in Chicago, we met a man on a plane. His name was Aladdin. We became good friends with Aladdin, and his girlfriend at the time, Mina. Of the many role models that Joe introduced me to, Tony Robbins became one of my beloved mentors shortly after meeting this couple. Mina, at the time was one of Tony's Peak Performance Strategists. She had countless hours of practice coaching and being trained by the best. Not only was this the summer that Joe and I were married by the "hugging saint," Amma, but the one when we attended Tony Robbin's weekend seminar Unleash the Power Within. My respect for Mina and her work with Robbin's Research International grew tremendously over a short period of time. Let's just say that I was a true raving fan. Mina is not only a dear friend, but an extraordinary life coach. When she came to visit us, we'd lived in California just over one year. I was struggling to find ground after moving from South Jersey, especially since I'd just began to feel as if I'd found my way there. I was giving Thai Massage sessions at home, leading weekly JourneyDance classes, teaching yoga, selling my art, and feeling I was truly living my passion. When we moved to California, everyone's mother, sister and brother seemed to be a yoga teacher. We moved into what felt like a shoebox compared to the town-home in May's Landing, and thus massage sessions in the house weren't an option. I didn't have my workshop to continue making jewelry and no one had heard of, or was interested in, JourneyDance. Hello Silicon Valley!

Mina wasn't having my defeatist story. Instead she directed the attention toward my strengths. "You know so much about nutrition and health, why don't you teach people?" Where this conversation led was to the potential of offering a service, much like the process I went through in Joe's kitchen, a few days after we'd met in South Jersey. There are thousands—maybe millions— of people just in the U.S. alone that could use a kitchen detox. I'm passionate about health, I love supporting people to discover their path to optimal health, and I've learned about health through decades of experience. Was this really me? Someone who comes in and tells you that 90% of the products in your kitchen are garbage?

As a reasonable estimate, well over half of my income was earned through exotic dancing for the previous six to eight years of my life. I'd heard it over and over in the personal development world, and it was hard to forget: ten thousand hours to mastery. Could it be that the only thing that I'd mastered in life was exotic dancing? At first consideration, this felt like somewhat of a curse. I thought to myself, "I'm in my late twenties and I've mastered a skill that's painstakingly unsustainable." I voiced my perspective to Joe when this seemingly dreary thought arose, expecting him to put a more positive spin on it. That he did. I've learned a plethora of invaluable skills in Gentlemen's clubs across the nation. Building rapport, communication and conscious listening, problem-solving, critical thinking, portraying self-confidence, techniques to captivate an audience, ability to perform on stage and in stilettos, trusting and understanding intuition—it's clear that the list is endless. I often feel that strippers should be awarded an experiential degree in psychotherapy. It was usual for me to take on the role of a coach, or therapist when I'd enter an hour or longer in the champagne room. My intention is always to give them something to potentially improve their lives. I'd attempt to discover what they felt was missing in their lives and help them see how to make the shift. The best exotic dancers are simply incredible listeners. Regardless of how each interaction moved forward and whether or not I played the therapist, I was left with a recurrent feeling that I'd just gone through another relationship. We'd meet, and decide we were a good fit. We'd try it out; spend some time together and engage in deep conversation. We'd break up when he decided that he wasn't able to financially support our relationship any longer, when a host would pop in the session and say, "time's up in about five minutes; would you like to spend more time with this beautiful lady?"

Each night was filled with a handful of micro-relationships. Years and years have accumulated into hundreds of these condensed relationships. I can't deny that I've learned a great deal about men and the dynamic of connection between masculine and feminine. This is certainly an unconventional route for learning about relationships, but nonetheless it has been legitimate experience. Even though these interactions I had in the club were just that; they were opportunities to experience the multitude of varied outcomes. The finesse that consistently resulted in what I thought of as success was what I recognize as sensuality.

It's not a skill that every exotic dancer seems to master, but I found the greatest pleasure in exploring the depth of sensuality. My understanding of sensuality is that it is a truly authentic expression of pleasure. The way that I connect with my own sensuality is very personal, as I believe it is for everyone. One way I can explain it is making love with myself. When I'm fully embodying sensuality, I am at peace and simultaneously in the rapture of pleasure. All of my senses are engaged and I perceive virtually everything external as desirable stimulation. For example, eating a simple piece of fruit, or a berry, becomes an entire experience. I feel a craving to draw out the pleasure. With my teeth, I puncture the flesh of a strawberry, and breathe deeply letting the aroma stimulate my palette while simultaneously allowing this orchestra of flavor dance with my taste buds. It's the art of slowing down and allowing, and it's a practice. Letting this practice become a shared experience, with a lover, is when things get really juicy.

Pleasure only deepens when two people join in experiencing sensuality together. Because of this belief, and implications it has with the culinary world, it only seems natural to connect with my lover in the kitchen. As I mentioned, Joe and I really began our relationship in the kitchen. The longer we mingle in the kitchen, and become more aware of our needs, the more we further refine our diet preferences. It's difficult to feel pleasure while eating packaged, processed "food" that isn't real or nutritious. When the things we're putting in our mouths are essentially dead, you can imagine what happens if we truly are what we eat. Experiencing pleasure through food is an incredible practice, but it doesn't work well if the food isn't really food. The dictionary definition for "food" most certainly includes the word "nourishment." Joe and I have spent countless hours investigating and learning about optimal nourishment. We want to feel our best, because it's a respectful act, and a responsibility—hence Joe's decision to kick the sugar addiction. If you're in a relationship and not taking care of yourself, what does that say to the other person? We're almost always adamant to make a drastic shift in our diet for the purpose of potentially feeling even more vibrant and energetic. There's so much more to offer to the relationship when conscious decisions are made; regarding what goes in (and even on) the sacred temple of the body.

Eliminating refined sugar from our lives was a challenge at first, but once we felt the benefit, there was no reason to go back; our decision was affirmed. Our dynamic of leading and following on this one was the real success. I LOVE sweets. Joe and I would dine out in the first few years of our relationship, and repeatedly encounter this scenario. We'd savor the last few bites, and the server would arrive with the dessert menu and ask, "Would you like to see the dessert menu?" Joe and would respond without missing a beat, "No thank you!" Simultaneously, I would respond, "Yes, of course." All it took was one conspiracy video that convinced Joe that he wasn't in control of his own biochemistry. I have to thank Joe on this one, because I wasn't strong enough at that moment to kick the habit. We're no longer addicted!

There's an insanely long list of little tweaks and shifts we've made in effort to move toward optimal health. This is a strong foundation that supports a conscious relationship. I won't say that if every couple mutually agrees to strive for optimal health that the relationship will thrive. However, I don't know how it will ever thrive without the fuel of real food AKA sensual food.

As it provides the necessary life force to feel amazing, and share that energy with a partner, the shift can be playful, fun, and simple. The incredible journey of becoming aware of what goes in and on this sacred temple—my body, has undoubtedly allowed more pleasure into my life. I highly recommend making love in your kitchen, on the path of conscious love.

How to Turn Conflict into Connection

Deborah Morehead

"Happiness, peace, love and acceptance comes through deep connection to yourself and to others.
Deep connection comes through conscious conflict when you remain curious and open. Only then will you create the amazing relationship you desire."
Deborah Morehead

Deeper connection through conflict IS possible!

Hurt, pain, sadness, loneliness and even despair are feelings we all have at times in our relationship with our significant other.

The question to ask is not, "How do I keep from having these feelings?", but, "What do I do with them when they show up?".

These feelings show up when we feel our needs are not being met within the relationship. Conflict arises when the needs of both people, while both important, happen to clash.

The answer isn't avoidance. Ignoring the feelings or the conflict never solves anything. The answer is in how you create deeper connection through the conflict. Yes! This is possible; even if it is not what you were taught or what was role modeled for you growing up.

So let's dive into the BIG QUESTION: how do you turn conflict into connection?

In this chapter I will lay out the necessary knowledge and skills you must have in order to move successfully into conflict and create a deeper connection with yourself and your significant other.

Let's start with the 'unconscious mate selection' process. Then I'll show you the necessary knowledge and skills to develop in order to be in control of yourself so you get more of what you want in your relationships. The #1 priority for maneuvering through the complexities of relationships and conflict is self-awareness. Then I'll share the exact conscious mindset to develop for successful relationships. Finally we will walk through the Conflict to Connection Cheat Sheet. This is a vital part of my Happy Relationship Success System. The Conflict to Connection Cheat Sheet will be your powerful companion through a step by step process you and your significant other can utilize to move successfully through conflict and create deeper connection.

Mate Selection
Why do we pick the partner that we pick? Mate selection is primarily done on the unconscious level. Unconsciously the people we are naturally drawn to have some of the strengths of our parents (or primary caregivers) AND the weaknesses.

Once you're in the relationship, you unconsciously begin to look for ways the other person either does or doesn't meet your needs. When the other person doesn't meet your needs, you react. The ways you react are ways you learned to cope with frustrations and hurts as a child as role-modeled by your parents.

Here's where those weaknesses of each person's parents play out. Your way of reacting reflects the weakness of your partner's parents. A negative cycle begins. The way you react to them not meeting your needs becomes a trigger for their unmet needs. And off the two of you go, round and round in a negative spiral downward consistently missing the other person's needs and disconnecting more and more with each round.

This is the pattern that happens time and time again when we play at an unconscious level. This is the reason the divorce rate is so high. Believe it or not your reactions actually unconsciously train the other person (because of their wounds and unmet needs) to treat you in a way that confirms your biggest fear, that you will never get your needs met.

Ryan sat stiffly in my office with a somewhat cold and stoic demeanor while Melissa, with tears running down her face, explained that she felt Ryan had left the marriage and that in recent past weeks he was spending more time at work than before and she had suspicions and concerns regarding how much time he was spending with one of his co-workers.

Ryan finally spoke up with anger in his voice to say Melissa had been sleeping in the spare bedroom for the last four months and that they had not had sex for more than six months. At this point both Melissa and Ryan had so much hurt, anger and disconnection that they both questioned whether they should even stay together.

To figure out how they got to this place let's start by looking at how they unconsciously chose one another. The strengths of Melissa's parents included a sense of being there for her, being loving, hardworking and having a sense of humor, all strengths that Ryan had as well. The weaknesses that Melissa's parents had included being critical, being complacent when it came to conflicts, distance and being prone to outbursts of anger, all weaknesses that Ryan had as well. The strengths of Ryan's parents included being loving, hard-working, spiritual, and having a sense of humor, all strengths that Melissa had. The weaknesses of Ryan's parents were being controlling, being critical and cutting off in silence, similar weaknesses that Melissa had as well.

Your unmet needs come from an emotional wound in your childhood. There was some sort of a consistent pattern of interacting with one or both of your primary caregivers which you experienced as consistently missing what you felt you needed emotionally. This is not about blaming your parents but understanding where your unmet needs came from so that you now have the ability to understand and shift it.

Melissa was a middle child of five children while growing up, and her mother often dealt with her frustrations with a lot of yelling, throwing things and hitting. Melissa's unmet needs and what she wanted more than anything else in a relationship were to be good enough, accepted and to experience calm. For Ryan, a second child, his father was extremely overprotective, often not allowing Ryan to do any of the normal childhood activities. Because Ryan's wants and feelings were often ignored his unmet needs became that he wanted to know he was understood and important.

How Melissa learned to deal with frustration and unmet needs as a child was to people-please from an anxious place without really understanding the feelings or needs of the other person while trying to get "it" right, criticizing herself and the other person when it wasn't right, giving up and ultimately cutting off in silence. Now look closely at the weaknesses of Ryan's parents. Do you see how Melissa's behaviors would have a familiar feeling to Ryan? Feeling controlled by her people-pleasing without really being seen, feeling criticized if at any point he spoke up and said he wanted something different, and eventually feeling emotionally abandoned by her cutting off. Also, look at Ryan's needs to feel important and understood. Would Melissa's behaviors make Ryan feel those needs were being met? No. So let's look at how Ryan would react.

How Ryan learned to deal with frustration and unmet needs as a child was just to comply and do what he was told to do, be silent, throw a fit when he would get really fed up, be angry, and when all else failed to give up and leave. Now look at the weaknesses of Melissa's parents. Again, Ryan's behaviors would leave Melissa with a familiar feeling from her childhood, feeling the complacency (no one will stand up for her so she has to do it all), feeling criticized, experiencing anger directed at her, and emotional distance by his emotional or physical disconnection.

Remember, Melissa's needs are to feel she is good enough and accepted and to have calm. So once again Ryan's behaviors would create a feeling in Melissa that her needs do not matter.

Let's look at it all put together:

Melissa becomes
defensive & critical
then cuts off in anger

Melissa becomes anxious
to please; anxiously does
this without connection
to the other person's
true needs

Ryan becomes
critical & demanding
because things were
not how he wanted it

Ryan has fits of anger
then gives up and
emotionally leaves

Figure 1

To help you move to a more conscious way of mate selection as well as relating within a relationship, here are four steps in my Happy Relationship Success System that you can do for yourself.
1. Identify the strengths and weaknesses of your primary caregivers
2. Identify 1 or 2 of your unmet needs
3. Recognize your ways of reacting from your childhood hurts and frustrations
4. Look for the lazy 8 pattern in your present or past relationships

Picking a mate from an unconscious place and playing out the relationship unconsciously gets you nowhere. You end up causing your own pain and the pain and hurt in your significant other as well. Once you bring your needs and your ways of relating to your conscious awareness you begin to increase connection. Then you'll be able to approach conflict from a different perspective.

The next step to moving into more conscious relationships begins with self-awareness and developing the skills in order to control and manage yourself first. This is the ONLY way to learn to maneuver successfully through the complexities of relationships and conflict.

Think about how many times you have lost control and ended up saying and doing things in your relationships that you wish you hadn't done. It is possible to learn how to control yourself.

Control Yourself First

When you live from an unconscious place you allow yourself to be a victim of life circumstances. You believe you feel how you feel because of what "they" said or did. You believe the negative thoughts in your head are true and that you have a right to ruminate on them because of what the other person said or did. A more conscious way of living means you shift from a reactive victim position into a proactive empowered position.

When you choose to live from a proactive empowered state you create your own happiness and learn how to connect more deeply even through conflict. You can do this by learning how to control your feelings and your thoughts.

Let's Start with Controlling Your Feelings.
Feelings are present for a reason. There is no such thing as wrong feelings. Feelings are there to tell you something. However, it is all about what you do with your feelings that matters.

It will help to start with understanding what's going on in your brain and body in order for you to control your feelings better.

We all have a caveman brain in us. Your brain is made up of three different sections. You have a hindbrain, midbrain and the prefrontal cortex. The hindbrain is instinctual and is all about reactions and the midbrain is about emotions. These two parts of your brain work together. Once something happens and your brain reads it as a threat your hindbrain reacts and your midbrain adds feelings. These parts of your brain have no concept of time; they react in order to survive and protect you, and once triggered communicate to glands to send out hormones and chemicals such as adrenaline and cortisol in order to move you into fight, flight or freeze action.

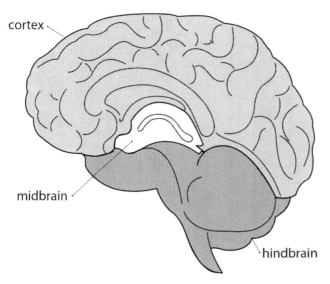

Figure 2

When saber-tooth tigers rustled in the bush your hind and mid parts of your brain helped you survive. Today, you don't live in a survival environment but your brain still works from that place. Your brain constantly looks for any possible dangers to you personally or emotionally.

Here are some examples of present day situations your brain reads as possible attacks: your boss criticizes you, a co-worker talks over you at a meeting, a driver cuts you off on the freeway, a friend doesn't acknowledge you when you walk into a party, your partner accuses you of doing something wrong, your partner treats you in a way that you experience as not meeting your needs, etc. The list can go on and on, right?

So what can you do about it if your brain and body are just doing what they are supposed to do?

The first step is to recognize your feelings, your body's reactions, and then control and manage yourself before doing anything else.

When your brain thinks it's in danger several things are happening inside of you. In your brain a lot of the blood and oxygen are flowing to your hind and midbrain so they can do their job. Your hind and midbrain are telling your glands to put out adrenaline and cortisol. When all this is going on the front part of your brain, the part that thinks rationally, is offline. So your first and only goal is to calm yourself down and get the extra hormones and chemicals out of your body.

You can live from a conscious empowered place when you learn to control your feelings. To do this you need to recognize when a negative feeling is triggered and then use calming techniques to get yourself back in control of your own feelings.

Here are a few researched and established techniques to calm the red hot parts of your brain and to wash the hormones out of your body.

• Deep Belly Breathing. Make sure you are breathing deeply into your lungs. The reason it is called belly breathing is because when done correctly your diaphragm expands as you fill your lungs and your belly extends outward. As you breathe deeply, count. Counting will help you to stop your negative thinking. Slowly breathe in to the count of five and out to the count of six. This is my favorite method of calming because you can use it anytime, anywhere.
• Progressive Muscle Relaxation created by Edmund Jacobson is another method of relaxation. This method is all about tensing and relaxing your muscles. The long version of this is to progress through muscle groups by tensing muscles and holding for several seconds and then completely relax. There is an entire process to do this with all muscle groups (start with your foot muscles, move to calf, then to thigh, etc.). A shorter version

that I often teach children is to tense all body muscles and then relax. The interesting thing is that when you are tensing and relaxing your muscles you are very present which allows you to calm yourself down.
• Any form of meditation or guided imagery has been proved to calm your brain and get your body back to normal.

Remember, you are the only person that can be in charge of your own feelings. No matter how much you believe you have the right to be angry you always have the choice in those moments to cause more damage and hurt to yourself, the other person and the relationship or to calm yourself. When you take charge and empower yourself by calming yourself you no longer have to be victim of your circumstances or what others say or do.

Once you have calmed yourself the second step is to look at your negative thoughts around the situation and learn how to be in control of your thoughts.

If your brain's job is to protect you then the thoughts it comes up with must be true. Right? Or is it?

We all have automatic negative thoughts. Your negative thoughts are your brain's job trying to help you to survive when it thinks you're under attack. Your brain believes its thoughts are the truth and are there to protect you.

Knowing that, you can be the one in charge of your thoughts. You can change your thoughts since you are the one creating them and therefore you can be in control of them. If you want to live from a conscious place, not be a victim to circumstances, and learn to create connection through conflict first learn to calm and be in control of negative feelings and then learn to identify and be in control of your thoughts.

Start by paying attentions to your negative thoughts. In difficult situations your job is to slow down and stop yourself before you react. Do this by paying attention to your feelings, taking a timeout (bathroom break) to calm yourself before you say and do things you will regret later. Once you have calmed yourself you can look at the negative thoughts that were driving your feelings.

Remember, a thought is only a story you tell yourself. It's your perception. The way we work as human beings is this; once you tell yourself that story, you believe it is true. And therefore you start looking for proof that your truth (story) is true.

In order to be in control of your thoughts you need to start to question them. Challenge your thoughts. Your brain came up with the thought to protect you but your negative thoughts end up working against you. Here are two of my favorite cognitive behavioral therapy questions to ask:

1. Is this thought 100% accurate?

2. Is this thought helpful for me?

If the answer is "no" to even one of these two questions then you know it is a negative thought. You are letting this negative thought have control over you, control over your happiness as well as any positive results you want within your relationship.

The third step is to change your thought. You can learn to catch the negative thought and change it. The idea of re-framing is to choose consciously to change the way you see things (your thought, your story). Once you do this you can begin to look for the evidence to prove this new story as true. If you are going to tell yourself a story, why not tell it so it is in your favor?

Here are a few tips to re-frame a thought:
1. Challenge the thought with the two questions so that your mind becomes open to other possible ways to think about the situation.
2. Find ways to bring in compassion for yourself and for the other person. What might be their experience or perspective?
3. Use milder or softer language. For example, "She never thinks about me or cares what is important to me," to "In this situation it seemed she didn't care about me, but other times she has shown she cared."
4. Think about what you might gain or learn from the situation.

Let's look at Melissa from our earlier story as an example of how learning to manage your feelings and thoughts can work to your advantage.

Melissa was naturally having very strong, reactive feelings regarding the situation with Ryan and his co-worker. Earlier in the year at Ryan's business Christmas party Melissa had met the co-worker. So she often had images that went with her thoughts about Ryan talking with his co-worker, and of course, she felt threatened, and got very angry when those thoughts came to her mind.

Prior to coming in to see me she had reacted to her thoughts by yelling at Ryan and on a few occasions she threw and broke things in the house. Now you may be thinking she had every right to act this way. She certainly had every right to feel her feelings of betrayal and anger.

As I helped Melissa to learn to take a timeout, breathe and calm herself, she began to experience in herself a level of confidence and self-love because she was now controlling her feelings which then allowed her, through the Conflict to Connection Cheat Sheet, to share her feelings, fears and needs and actually experience Ryan understanding her and moving towards her.

Problems occur when you remain in your angry state and direct your reactive behaviors at the other person. By doing this you actually create the opposite of what you want and end up pushing them away. When you manage your feelings and then have the skills to dialogue effectively you actually create deeper connection.

When Melissa and I looked at the variety of her negative thoughts and re-framed them she shifted many of her thoughts which then allowed her to move forward in the relationship with Ryan and both of them were able to build and create deeper connection and a new more improved relationship.

Here are a few of the re-frames:

1. "He's had sex with her" to "I don't know if he has had sex with her, I choose to trust his words."
2. "He doesn't love me anymore" to "He is still here and working on this relationship so he does love me."
3. "I can't be with someone who has cheated on me" to "He understands why he started talking to her and he continues to grow" and
4 "He has ruined our marriage" to "We have both made hurtful mistakes and this was a wake-up call to create something amazing."

Please note both Melissa and Ryan had been hurt, had lots of big negative feelings and both were experiencing tons of negative thoughts that were keeping them stuck when they first came to see me. In this situation Ryan had a variety of his own thoughts and feelings keeping him stuck that were shifted as well. Keep in mind there is an entire process to helping a couple work through any sort of infidelity that I have short cut in this example.

Now that you are beginning to think from a more conscious empowered and self-aware place let's spend some time talking about a more effective mindset around conflict as well as a conscious mature way to think about love.

Conflict Mindset and Mature Love
Why is it that most of us have no problem handling our upsets at work and yet we think it is perfectly fine or even necessary to just let our messy feelings and words out all over our significant other? Why is it okay to treat the most important people in our lives this way? To have a successful relationship you need to start protecting what is most precious to you. At work you contain it because you know to survive you need to keep your job. If you can do this at work isn't it even more important to do it with your significant others in your life? Use your skills in controlling your feelings and thoughts from above so that you protect and learn to create the connection you desire.

"IT'S YOU AND ME AGAINST THE PROBLEM." This mindset becomes imperative if you want to move more consciously into conflict and connect more deeply. This mindset will protect the relationship. Think about it; when you feel under attack because of a criticism or accusation you automatically shift to a stance of me against the other person. You begin to defend yourself and attack the other person. This always creates more hurt and damage in the relationship. So hold "IT'S YOU AND ME AGAINST THE PROBLEM" attitude.

There are so many different ways we love throughout our lifetime. When we are infants and toddlers we know only how to have a selfish love. Think of a two-year-old. You want it your way and you want it now. Love from this place doesn't take the other person into account and will eventually end a relationship. Another type of love is quid pro quo love. This love is, "I will love you if you love me." This kind of love is always keeping tabs. It is an attitude of, "If you do your part in the relationship then I'll do my part." Love from this place is never satisfying because it is always looking for what isn't being done. Eventually each person is more and more hurt and more and more withholding. So what kind of love do you want to hold? Unconditional love. As human beings no one is perfect at this, but the more you hold unconditional love for yourself and for those in your life the happier you will feel within yourself and the more love you will bring to those around you. When you are cut off from unconditional love you don't feel it within yourself and then you go into survival mode and revert to demanding love or quid pro quo. I know this will not always be easy but I encourage you to make it a conscious practice in your life. You will be amazed at how you will feel when you more consistently live from unconditional love.

Now that you understand why you have picked the mate you have chosen, understand your unmet needs and your mate's unmet needs, know how to better control your thoughts and feelings, and you have a shifted mindset around conflict and love you can move into creating connection through conflict.

Conflict to Connection Cheat Sheet
When you use the Conflict to Connection Cheat Sheet you will experience that connecting is possible even in conflict.

Every one of us wants to be understood and wants the other person to hear and agree with our perspective. The problem when it comes to conflict is that your caveman brain is stuck on thinking you need to protect yourself. So you end up believing you HAVE to get the other person to understand and accept your point of view. But the opposite is actually true. Instead of insisting the other person understands you; start with the desire to understand the other person. We all experience hurt, pain and misunderstanding and we all long for understanding, love and connection. When conflict arises remind yourself to be compassionate and curious first. Compassion and curiosity will move you towards deeper connection. So manage your own feelings and thoughts, shift to the position of, "You and me Against the Problem," put your perspective temporarily on the shelf and be curious and compassionate towards the other person. Connection isn't in being right, winning or getting the other person to give up their viewpoint. Connection is made when you can step into the other person's perspective so that deeper understanding is created. Therefore, go into the conversation holding compassion and curiosity. Then you can use the Conflict to Connection Cheat Sheet to help you create deeper connection and understanding in any conflict.

The Conflict to Connection Cheat Sheet is a step by step structure that guides you successfully through conflict into connection and understanding. The process includes two roles; speaker and listener. The speaker's job is to thoroughly and accurately express their perspective. This is done in a non-attacking or judging manner. Additionally, the expression is done from a vulnerable place of sharing feelings and connecting to any possible similar experiences from their past. Connecting to the past experiences becomes important because often the bigger the emotional response the more likely it is connected to a past or childhood experience. It is the speaker's responsibility to ensure the listener thoroughly understands all aspects of their feelings, experience and ways of thinking about the problem. The role of the listener is to hear and understand the speaker's perspective in a non-reactive manner. To do this the listener uses active listening including paraphrasing, empathy and validation and asks questions only in order to help the speaker express themselves and get clarity on any aspect the listener has not come to full understanding.

The speaker's role includes:

1. Using I statements. "I" statements include how you feel and describe factually (not blaming or judging) the actions of the other person. For example, "I feel resentful and frustrated, because this is the fourth week in a row that I have taken the trash out to the garbage can."
2. Appreciation. As human beings we like to hear praise or appreciation for the positive that we have done. For that reason when the speaker begins, whenever possible, state an appreciation regarding something positive you have seen or experienced the listener doing or attempting to do regarding the topic that you are talking about. In our example the speaker could say, "I want you to know I have appreciated the times you have taken the trash out in the past." If you aren't able to come up with an appreciation around the topic you can begin the conversation by saying, "I really appreciate you taking the time to hear my concern."

The listener's role includes:

1. Thorough understanding. In order to thoroughly understand the other person's perspective the listener must be able to listen actively, mirror back what they are hearing, utilize empathy and validate what they are hearing. All of these elements allow the speaker to experience that they are being understood and will help the listener to come to a true understanding of what the speaker is trying to communicate.

There is a joke about a teacher who is really upset with a student and the student says, "You are mad at me." The teacher says, "No I'm not mad." The student says back, "Then you should tell your face that." lol!

Active listening includes paying attention to your tone of voice, your facial expressions and your body stance. When you are listening actively you respond in positive manners, make eye contact, give nods, uh-hums, get rid of any distractions, and not be thinking about your rebuttal (you will have your chance to be speaker later, you can jot notes to get those thoughts out of your head and so you can remember them when it is your turn later). You ask open ended questions for more complete understanding (in the Conflict to Connection Cheat Sheet there is a list of examples of open ended question you can utilize), including mirroring, empathy and validating statements.

Mirroring is the idea of paraphrasing what you are hearing from the speaker. For example, "You feel resentful and frustrated that you have been the one to take the trash out for the last four weeks." Then check in with the speaker to make sure you got it right. Continue until the speaker experiences you completely understanding the point being discussed.

In the Conflict to Connection Cheat Sheet empathy and validation are an integral part of the listener's role. Empathy is the ability to feel what the other person is feeling in that situation. It is the ability to step into their shoes and imagine how you would feel and what you might think in the situation. Validating statements mean you are saying to the other person that it makes sense and that you agree with or accept what they are saying.

Here is an example of an empathetic and validating statement, "What you are saying makes sense to me because if I had taken the garbage out four weeks in a row I'm sure I would feel frustrated and resentful too."

2. Agreement. Once the speaker experiences that they have shared all they needed to share regarding the topic and felt that the listener understands their perspective then the listener wants to make statements as to what they agree about regarding what has been said. Agreement is an important step towards connection. Remember, just because you agree with portions of what the speaker has said does not mean you are giving up your perspective. It just means you are connecting to their perspective. At this point you share the areas that you agree on. It could be that you agree on the facts, feelings, ideas and/or perceptions of the speaker.

Depending on what the conflict is about there may need to be a final step of collaboration and problem solving. This occurs only once both people have been in the speaker role and have experienced feeling understood. Conflict to Connection Cheat Sheet covers the last steps of collaboration when required. In many instances once there is a connection around being heard and understood there may be only a need for understanding and apology on one or both person's part.

For Melissa and Ryan it took eleven months of helping each person to connect to their family of origin patterns that were playing out, consistent accountability for each of them to look at and manage their own feelings and thoughts, and one hundred plus Conflict to Connection Cheat Sheet conversations both in the office and at home for them to create compassion, deep connection and to build a new stronger loving and happy relationship that they both had always desired.

Conflict is a normal part of relationships. But it doesn't have to end in despair and hurt. Deeper connection is possible when you are willing to look at and understand the way your unconscious is playing out in the relationship, control yourself first, hold your significant other and the relationship as precious with the mindset of us against the problem, and consistently utilize the Conflict to Connection Cheat Sheet format for successful connection through conflict. You can find the Conflict to Connection Cheat Sheet and a guide here http://blisslifepress.com/conscious-love/bonuses/

50 Shades of Conscious Sexuality: The Cosmic Dance of Sex, Love, and Awakening

Christopher Menné

"Spiritually oriented people often need to realize the true and higher nature of sexuality in their lives, and not doing so can often be a terribly diminishing experience. As free as we are today to pursue choices on sex, coupling, and love, higher sexual intelligence and life-giving sexual energies often remain unrealized. To be open to higher sexual intelligence and sexual energy IS naturally more erotic and loving. And we can also come to see that from a higher perspective, such empowered sexuality can fuel authentic spiritual awakening, and support the higher-consciousness that wants to come into the world today."
Christopher Menné

In the first half of my life, through my mid 30s or so, when it came to sex and love, like many I thought I knew what I wanted. I was becoming increasingly aware of the subtle relational knowledge and expanded sexual skills that could make big differences in both choosing partners and having relationships. But, it wasn't until I unexpectedly became a parent that all this changed.

Ah, I really thought I knew, through and through, what I wanted. What follows is my sometimes painful, often awkward, frequently humbling, and ultimately liberating journey to locate what it takes to "not know" what I want, but to know how to align with the infinite truths of sex and love. And this alignment is always deepening. Simply said, I did not know what I did not know.

Indeed I had spent a lot of sincere time and energy with partners, patiently becoming aware of the skillful and delicate nature of becoming a competent lover. I was also opening to the complexities of how we choose partners, and somewhat repeat, to varying degrees, patterns of relating and giving and receiving love based on our childhood influences.

There was both confusion and joy at this time, because the conception occurred with a woman who was diagnosed as being infertile. That was surprise number one, because we had been quite comfortable, even looking forward to being together without the premise of having children. Surprise number two was that our relationship was beginning to reveal some significant difficulties— give or take some variables, and what led to the pregnancy was essentially drawn-out 'break up sex' between a supposedly infertile couple. As you might imagine, one of our many conversations was, "Omg! Now what will we do?"

Fast-forward almost 20 years. After deciding to not be a couple, and choosing to co-parent even before our daughter was born, we have raised a daughter who has grown into a young woman who is thriving. Our daughter is a straight 'A' student on her way to college, an accomplished dancer and musician who is popular with friends and wise beyond her years in her own relationships. This is possible because she has never doubted how much she is loved. As she has come to understand the nuances and delicate nature of attraction, sex and love, she is fully aware of, and proud of, her origins. She is proud of her parents who were wise enough to not marry, and who keep showing up 100%. Her mom has since married, and all three of our daughters' parents get along well, and work hard at making solid decisions together. We trust each other, all four of us.

There is so much more to say about this scenario with our daughter. However, what follows is a story of my exploration of what it takes to know one's self, and fully share one's self when loving someone, as well as fully receiving someone who is loving me. This exploration was driven in part by the sudden 'wake-up call' of having a child in the midst of a difficult relationship. Although we showed up to co-parent fully, joyfully, and deeply, I had a strong feeling I had much to learn about how to form and contribute to a love relationship with fewer challenges and more resources. There was even a sense of personal pain related to the feeling that I was missing some core understanding, or way of Being. I also felt somewhat driven to be able to share someday with our daughter, if she ever asked, who I was when she was conceived, and who I have grown to be, or maybe who I have even woken-up to be. What this all led me to I really could not have imagined in my 30s (although I sense this sort of realization is available at any age). I learned I needed to deeply discover who I was as a sexual being, develop solid self-awareness as a person, and to establish some real tangible or felt spiritual awareness.

As elementary as this may sound, it is so true; to know one's self is the basis of being able to trust one's self, and therefore, leads to trusting yourself in loving another. This is also the basis of learning to understand another, to see outside one's self to see another as they are, and trust them in loving you. Little did I know, this is lifetime work.

I have always been somewhat of a mystical seeker, quite curious about our essential or spiritual nature. As mentioned previously, even prior to becoming a parent, I had been getting really interested in the nuances of both sex and enhanced relationship dynamics. All this merged and grew over 20 years, some of which you will see on these pages.

An entire book could be written about my journey of the last 20 years as I explored the heart and truth of the relationship between sex and spirituality, and how our personal sense of self works with all this. I have come to see that as we release ourselves from the conditioning of society, and impressions of how we were loved (or not) as children, there is a core intelligence each person has that can be a guide to how they will be fulfilled in loving and being loved. We can uncover and discover this core intelligence, and then cultivate it if we desire. As for what I am sharing here, there are core common truths about how human beings function as sexual and loving beings, and significant essential truths about our spiritual nature as well. I now make a living supporting singles and couples in becoming well acquainted and empowered with their most core sexual nature, while becoming clear with their spiritual sense of self or their Higher-Self, and how to join our sexual self and Higher-Self to attract and create extraordinary relationships.

By-the-way, I can clearly see I might have wound up in this field of contribution, with or without my becoming a parent. However, I believe my experience as a parent has had a lot to do with it! In fact, I used to be an airline pilot, and then shortly after my daughter's birth, I went back to Graduate School to study Psychology, Consciousness, and Spirituality. And yes, the fact that I met my daughter's mom as a flight attendant, while we were working, adds to the sweet drama and richness of our story, and to our daughter's fine and truly authentic legacy. It is almost as if our daughter chose us. But that is another book . . .

Today, the term 'Conscious Sexuality' includes a wide range of considerations on sex and love. Mostly, we think of how to improve our experiences of sex, and/or how to become more available for love; as well as how to address the challenges that can arise with intimacy. As we can see with every chapter in this book, there are many fine ways to bring more to how we experience, express, receive, and share sex and love, as well as for how to handle the challenges that will arise.

It is often our egoic sense of self we are working on, when we make positive changes in our behavior; changes which can embrace improved and more-knowledgeable relational and sexual techniques.

Ego health, psychological health, relational skills, seeing the impact of our childhood has on us today, attachment considerations and the like; these are what we can all have in the mix, and are elements that can hold us back from having fuller experiences of sex and love. When addressed properly, this is all important, good and worthwhile work, and can be very satisfying, too.

As challenges are addressed, and the improvements that have been sought after regarding sex and love start to become available, if you are a 'seeker' or one who is committed to a path of personal growth, you may have periods where you become aware of the following:

It can sometimes feel as if you are outgrowing your sense of self. When it comes to sex and love, this can get a little tricky. Once this occurs, we come to see that our relative sense of self, or our ego self, was the 'who' that was having our relationships. It is our very sense of who we are which is shifting. The ego is becoming lighter, a little more transparent, and a broader sense of self is emerging. It is important to note that this is not a problem, but a shift.

If you have come up against this you know it is true. Professionally and personally, I can attest to this "shift" in consciousness. When it begins to show up, this can be the adventure of a lifetime. Single or partnered, sex and love take on an entirely different place in life. Less ego attachment is in play, less fear, more satisfying sex, more authenticity, and an expansive sense of love.

Experiences of sex and love which are felt both viscerally and spiritually.

This concept will be revisited again throughout this chapter, but for now let's imagine your sex drive... feel your sex drive. Allow for sexual desire to arise. If it's erotic, that is okay, but go deeper. Where does it come from? Your body? Your genitals? Or is it a drive to be in union with another? Whatever it is, FEEL IT. Go deep. Without thought or fantasy, just feel. Look deeper, feel the motivation, not the need, but tap into the drive. Now ask. Where does this originate? Keep asking that question, as you close your eyes for a little while, and then continue on this journey with me...

Okay, now you have experienced that which is the felt nature of our sex drive. It has a non-physical root. Our sexual desire has a non-physical origin. Feel this. Imagine being able to bring this to your lovemaking.

And about love... we see that love is not something to attain; love is always there when we are moving and relating with more Being, and less ego. This is something that once you have experienced, you know firsthand, the experiential ground of Being is love. When we share our Being, we are therefore "in love" together. This is the felt nature of higher love, which emanates from Being.

These are the more 'felt' and 'conscious' experiences with sex and love, that we will continue to explore in this chapter. This can begin directly to fuel spiritual awakening. The depth of connection you can feel with another can be astounding.

Recall for a moment, your early teens or twenties. What it was like as you were becoming accustomed to the physicality of your own maturing body and sexual response, and to that of the bodies of lovers and partners you were with, and the significance of becoming a lover— the skills, understandings and comfort levels you strove for? As you did so, your natural sexual drive could flourish within the skills, understandings, and comfort levels with the sexual capacities you internalized. This was a paradigm shift, which resulted from your physical sexual maturation; you were becoming a fully sexual person in the conventional sense of the word. This move toward a broader sense of experience and consciousness with sex and love is also a paradigm shift, a paradigm shift of similar, if not greater, magnitude. We'll see why as we continue here.

This is a natural next step with sex and love for conscious and spiritually inclined individuals. And in fact, this is a natural next step for any human whose consciousness is growing or evolving.

It is easy to miss this opening for a few reasons. One, it easy to assume we are "complete" in our internalizations of sex and sexual experience, when in actuality our sexual experience and capacity is somewhat unlimited, and can touch the transcendent. Another is a sort of mild protectiveness that many of us carry around our sexual sense of self that, "I've got this," and, "I know how to love and be loved," when in actuality, we are often unknowingly defending our limitations. Why? Because what is familiar is often comfortable, perhaps not fulfilling, but comfortable.

As mentioned, when I was in my late 30s, I hit this paradigm shift, and my initial resistance to it. Having gotten through the resistance, almost 20 years later, this life-giving shift is still underway. In fact, it never ends; it is somewhat of an opening to the infinite.

In the early days of this shift, as I was becoming more self-aware, and was involved with more self-aware partners, I had some really difficult experiences. The shifts toward more consciousness in life were showing up, but in relationship, persistent egocentric behavior and roles were still in place. At first this was baffling and painful to me. Then I saw some patterns:

After growing through the work and fulfillment of having good sexual and emotional needs met, sharing similar outlooks on life, being there for each other, and even getting pretty good at conflict resolution and the like, now and then some gaping chasms would show up out of nowhere. Or worse, sex and love would become a habit, leading to less feeling of being alive and less connection. Ouch.

Being somewhat of a fan of the more mystical aspects of life, I asked, "What makes sex so interesting and satisfying at times and others times less so? What is self-awareness and sense-of-self, and how does love arise at times to fill the hearts between partners, and other times fade, etc.?" Over the years, I came to see how the felt origins of sex and love can be directly nurtured via two experiential paths which are as natural to embrace and embody as making love itself, once we realize they exist:

•   Knowledge of sexual energy (which requires some solid anatomical sexual skills). This involves a higher-awareness of the experience or perception of the sex you are having, and how this can open

your sense of Essential Presence or Being— while becoming aware of
sexual energies.
    •   Cultivating this higher-sense-of-self, your Essential Presence
or Being— and how to share this as increasing degrees of authentic
sexual-love and connection become available. This can induce a big shift in
your experience of love.

Really, what is all of this? That was my take when I really dived into this
domain. What I learned is that there is a lot of useful and solid material
available such as physical sexual skill, tantric skills with sexual energy,
psychological health, and information on the awareness of the Higher-Self.

What I also found was this; as people grow and start practicing things like
mindfulness and meditation— good sex, comfortable love and
companionship can, increasingly, not be enough to hold the relationship
together. This stems not from a perspective of relationship problems, but
from a longing for more than comfort or even the desire for improvement.
This is a more authentic desire for a deeper and higher connection that we
know can arise. We sense, or know directly, that this is more than ego
based. We long for connection with another that is more deeply woven
with the physical, and for such physicality to be more intimate, when
merged with higher-consciousness or the spiritual.

"Oh, this is about how to manifest a soul-mate," you might be saying.

Not really. What I am referring to here is not something to do, or how to
get something— it is a way to be. A way to be, which allows you enter into
the flow of life, a river of life force which wants fulfillment for you, and all
women and men, in any kind of sexual-love relationship that they desire.
If it is a soul mate you desire, then yes, soul mate it is. Whatever it is you
desire, more essential experiences of sex and love will be part of your
journey.

I also found well-researched but little known understandings which
indicate that as we mature or evolve our consciousness, we 'need' and
want better sex— transcendent sex. The same goes for more love.

We 'need' more love — a higher love from a higher sense of self.

This IS why needs and interests regarding sex and love begin to shift—
there is a higher need, a spiritual need— that is not getting met. This is
natural. Unfortunately, these embodiments around sexual-love are all too
rare in our society, and quite honestly, in the world at large.

This is a natural shift where you come to see your ego as a sense of self,
which sort of rides in the middle, between the physical (sexual pleasure),
and the non-physical (the source of love). As an experience, you begin to
increasingly "see" your ego's interpretations of sex and love. You also
begin to see how much the ego had demanded in the past, thinking and

believing that its interpretations of sex and love were the real thing. As you become more and more aware of the ego, these limited or even false interpretations of sex and love become less and less interesting. You want the real thing. You want real sex and real love. You may also start having a more expanded experience of a sense-of-self which "sees" your ego, an ego which is simply forming representations of sex and love and often not experiencing sex and love, or even your partner, directly. At first this can be unsettling, but just like becoming familiar with your physical sexual anatomy as a teenager, with truth, understanding and support, the big 'YOU' (your higher sense of self) can begin 'watching' your ego. This is an opening to an entirely fresh dynamic of sex, love, and relationships. This new, higher perspective on sex and love is intrinsically more resourceful and alive, and tends not to become a habit or ever to grow old. Sometimes referred to as being ego-aware, this is an empowering step-up from self-awareness. Once you know this first-hand, you can also experience others who are becoming acquainted with becoming ego-aware. For those of you who are working with this, you know how exciting it can be. If this is new to you, and it interests you, know this is natural, and allow yourself to feel good about it. If you are drawn to these words, you are ready and this broader expression of sex and love will arise in your life.

Through following this high vibrational, ultimately more conscious impulse to experience sex and love more authentically (and with a lot more pleasure!), you are aligning with the aspiration of all the true spiritual teachings, which universally revere two paths. One of these paths is to "see reality as it is," with clear perception and less ego interpretation, and the other is to increasingly "see" the ego itself from a higher perspective or higher sense of self. Some call this higher sense of self their Being, Essence, Essential Presence, Higher-Self, Soul, Witness, Consciousness. Here we will use the terms Being, Essence, Essential Presence, and Higher-Self. A large discussion onto itself, but important to mention, is that experiencing life from this higher sense of self is also sometimes referred to as awakening.

This is a natural paradigm shift. Not unlike outgrowing our childhood bodies as we mature our physical sexuality, this is a shift of equal magnitude. As we outgrow an "ego-only" consciousness, we mature into a larger sense of self, which includes the ego, but is less and less defined by the ego. Less ego; more Being.

With the kind of work we provide, or through similar work , you can navigate this shift in consciousness on sex and love with more grace and ease. If these experiences and moments of awareness are coming up for you, and if you desire, you cannot only support this shift in consciousness, but induce it as well. That's right; you can raise your consciousness through re-framing your experience of sex and love — it goes both ways. This adds new meaning to the consideration that relationships can make us better people. These elevated forms of sex and love do contribute to the growth of your consciousness.

When you are ready, this can be the adventure of a lifetime!

There are many degrees or shades of this adventure of sex and love. Once familiar with this larger landscape, the living variability can become quite artful, as well.

I can say from my own experiences, and from working with others, the shift can be huge and profound: from simply meeting your needs, to training your attention and perception to fully see, feel and perceive your partner— your teammate— without filters or interpretations. This alone is huge! The words here are a bit abstract, but if you have ever felt "fully seen," you know how amazing it is. You can learn to "feel" the energy associated with Being in your heart area, and in and within your partner's heart area. This in and of itself is amazing, and so is the sex! This sort of clarified attention is also invaluable when single and meeting potential partners. The ability to cut artfully through pretense, to be authentic, to connect and to see clearly, is both powerful and attractive.

In this chapter we go right to the sensory core of the experience of sex. More than pleasure (although we look to cultivate huge pleasure), we look at the inherent spiritual root of sexual pleasure and sexual energy. We look at approaches to connect with core sexual pleasure and energy, and how to cultivate and amplify them to induce a sense of Essential Presence or Being. This will be equally weighted with an exploration of how increasing degrees of felt love can arise, as Being-to-Being connections are cultivated, through more practiced ways of being sexual.

To nurture these felt origins of sex and love, let's look more closely at these two core competencies, the two experiential paths mentioned earlier. We'll take an unflinching look into exploring how to touch and expand the core of our erotic experience. We will also look at some of the essential aspects of how our innermost self, our Higher-Self, or our Being, directly experiences love.

• One experiential path is the knowledge of sexual energy, which requires some solid anatomical sexual skills, as well. This involves a higher-awareness of the experience or perception of the sex you are having, and how this can open your sense of Essential Presence or Being, while at the same time, becoming aware of sexual energies.

Is tantra being discussed here? Yes, to a degree. But to be more precise, I am talking about a "full spectrum" competency with sexuality, which includes some core aspects of the sexual practice you could call "tantric." I am talking about techniques, as well, although this is really about sensation and perception. To simplify, the essential sexual practices, derived from tantra, and modern research on sexual response are:

• Extended periods of being sensual and having intercourse—

openness to raising capacity to experience increased physical sensation, feeling, and emotion.
• Delayed male climax, sometimes for days
• Cultivation of continuous female sexual stimulation with an openness to multiple female orgasm • Cultivate awareness of male/female polarities of sexual drive and sensation
• Utilization of the above to:
• Build and amplify sexual sensation to become aware of sexual energy associated with sexual pleasure
• Expand sexual energy to become aware of "subtle-body" energy (real, felt, and perceivable)
• Draw on, and direct felt subtle energy to expand consciousness

Implementing these practices can induce more Presence — a core sense of your Self, your Being. Genuine, altered states of consciousness, and even sustained higher states of consciousness, become available.

Intense experiences of heightened pleasure, and feeling deeply connected are common.

"What about my orgasm?" the guys say.

Not to worry, what you are experiencing here is, in many ways, better than orgasm. And when men do choose to climax, look out! Delayed male climaxing is a powerful event on many levels. Both partners are often deeply satisfied with the depth of sensation a woman's body can hold with such practice, and while staying present and available to her continued experience of being pleasured, and being open to orgasm. It is important to note that these practices, with natural adjustments, work equally well with same sex couples.

When we come to such a place of touching and opening our Essential Presence with someone else through such intentional sexuality, there is nothing else like this on the planet, except perhaps for a direct transcendent experience of God or the Universe, or sharing in the death or birth experience of another. I can share and tell you this from a place of authenticity, integrity and experience. In my body, heart, and from a core sense of self and awareness; in combination with what I have seen professionally; and what has been documented in mystical texts throughout the ages: I know this profound truth is our Birthright.

• The other experiential path is cultivating this higher sense of self, your Essential Presence or Being, and how to share this, as increasing degrees of authentic sexual-love and connection become available. This can induce a big shift in your experience of love.

Three degrees, or shades, of the experience of sexual-love follow below:

Our Core Longing for Sex
This is our basic drive to experience pleasure, explore attachment with another, and if it is the case, to reproduce. Sex at this level is about the satisfaction of a need. We feel desirous. We look for a means to satisfy our lust, and we experience release. There is a basic cycle of tension and release, and short-term satisfaction.

When this core physical level is present in a conscious, balanced and positive way, it adds a rich, lustful, earthy, gutsy, full-bodied experience to sex. As we explore the more refined levels of sexuality, this raw sexual experience is a powerful motivation to align with. It is not something to be let go or denied, but something to be embraced in awareness and transformed. We can begin to see honestly, that this physical drive is an engine that often draws us to one another, and an impulse which provides a robust vehicle to continue connecting to one another, once we are lovers or partners.

When the physical level is present in an unconscious and distorted way, sex tends to be brief, rough, genitally focused, and routine. The energies at play at this level are powerful, primal and when unexamined or unconscious, these energies are easily ensnared in porn, sex-based affairs and obsession toward and/or resistance to our natural sex drives. This can easily allow for objectification of who each person is, as someone to have, or be gratified with, at any more than a primal, physical level.

The Relational Experience of Sex, Love, and Intimacy
This is the level where sex becomes the expression of a personal sense of love and intimacy between two human beings. When this experience is present in a full and conscious way, sex can become lovemaking, slow and prolonged and sensual, with a wide expression of feeling from the intensely passionate to the light and playful. It's about giving and receiving flow together, and there is a deep connection of shared feelings and personal identities. Pleasure and pleasuring become more of a focus, rather than the satisfaction of immediate need. Physicality is fully present, and strong feelings of affection, attachment, and love can be experienced. We can feel free with our physicality too to see sexual attachment as good, strong, and enjoyable; and we can appreciate how it helps us to stay connected.

However, relational love is naturally somewhat egoic-oriented; childhood wounds, attachment issues, and our emotional needs and dependencies can get projected onto our partner. These projections are the unexamined and amplified ego-interpretations of another. For a conscious and open couple, such projections are a gift, because they offer the opportunity to grow in intimacy and self-awareness, and perhaps open the individuals and/or the couple up to the further experience of Being Based Love. However, when such projections remain unconscious, they can create a web of distortion and dependency that may suffocate and destroy the relationship. This is where counseling and therapy can be very supportive.

Aside from issues mentioned in the previous paragraph, problematic, egoic tendencies in relational love can arise because an ego is well, an ego. Even healthy egos often have a "What's in it for me" outlook and we can drift into sex and love which become mild "commodity swaps," and can be subject to "binary opposites," on-and-off. Here one day, utterly gone the next, depending upon the needs of the ego. Overall though, healthier, personal or relational love that is less ego driven can be resourceful, as well as a source of ease and comfort.

With relational love, we can begin to see degrees or shades of love. With compassion and an unwavering shared humanity, this must be said with honesty, we all often confuse lust (sex drive), attraction, attachment, and bonding, with love. This is perfectly normal and can even be fun, when we start to see and recognize all of these aspects of sex and love. However, we do want to be able to come to distinguish the HUGE difference between egoic driven love, healthy relational or personal love, and our Being's "felt love" which emanates from the spiritual realm. These differences can get a little blurry, but the personal truths of these distinctions do resonate with anyone who is interested in growing into and expanding into these fascinating and very real experiences.

The Being based experience of sex, love, and intimacy
This is sometimes described as sharing Essential Presence, or a Being-to-Being connection. This experience can arise out of the relational level at a time when an individual commits to a spiritual practice and/or consciousness work. Personal identity lightly falls away and the Higher-Self or pure Being emerges with a tangible sense of identity which is quite expanded and somewhat distinct from ego. (For those new to this, imagine or feel the part of you that has "always been there" from childhood until now— apart from memories— there is a timeless quality). There can also be an element of our 'mask' or role falling away, being more authentic, more direct. Partners can open to perceiving, feeling, and expressing from these broader aspects of self, and there can be profound union experienced beyond one's own sense of self. Somewhat beyond words, this is a total and direct experience of clear love. There can also be a lot playfulness and creativity shared here too.

Experiencing sexuality from Essence is not something you do; this is a state of Being. And true, even with no practice, it does arise. It is natural, and many have had such moments. Cultivating Essential Presence via the sound sexual practices and embodiments mentioned earlier is available to willing partners (and you can cultivate this experience without a partner too). Yet this is not something to achieve; rather we open to the profound practiced sensations and sexual energy we experience which can then induce our opening to Essential Presence. How it arises and to what degree is never up to us. As you deepen in your inner work, and as you let go of more and more ego attachment, contraction or fear, you surrender and open to a feeling of higher love which often accompanies our experiences of higher consciousness. With the proper context and truth-based practices, sexually activated Being or Essential Presence simply happens. It is natural.

Orientation to this level of sex and sexuality heals past wounds, supports higher functioning in life, and can fuel authentic spiritual awakening.

Robust physical and healthy relational levels are included, and freely experienced as part of the whole transcendent experience. Sometimes attention may gravitate toward powerful physical sex only, or profound experiences of relational love. All is welcome.

Spiritual love from Being, is a "State of Being" which has no opposite, and draws from an infinite source we can often directly feel when our consciousness opens to Essence. The "love" a couple experiences here is based in a "felt" sense of connection that naturally resonates between the spiritual love each partner is radiating. Much more robust than the transient "high" of egoic love, or even the "comfort" of personal love, shared Being based love "feels good" in a tangible, grounded, and sustainable way. We thrive. True, like all "States of Being," Being-based love may ebb and flow, as felt resonance can always change. However, Being-based love has no "opposite," no "love take-away," a common experience of problematic, egoic love. Being-based love also directly addresses the benign "habit" that even personal and healthy relational love can sometimes be challenged with over time.

There is no distorted, unconscious form of shared Essential Presence, but; there is a trap which is a form of "spiritual bypass." This is where we can create a fantasy form of Being-to-Being connection in our heads and act it out. We make everything appear beautiful. We speak fine and high words. We "spiritualize" our sex. However, unexamined aspects of physical and relational experiences can trip us up. A strong couple with sound understandings of themselves and one another can use such challenges as huge opportunities to deepen their connection and intimacy, and possibly explore more Being-to-Being connections.

This experience of Being-to-Being contact, and the pure love from higher consciousness that is accessed during such transcendent sex, increasingly impacts life outside of being sexual. We see that love is not something to attain; love is always there. This kind of transcendent sex and Being-to-Being connection gives us access to this omnipresent field of love that is often felt when we are moving and relating with more Being, and less ego. This is something that once you have experienced, you know first-hand; the ground of Essential Presence and Being is love. When we share our Being, we are therefore "in love" together. It is very different from the more common experiences of being-in-love, and yet it does not deny healthy aspects of physical and relational love. This Being-based experience of love often results in life-changing insights, where the felt sense of love that we touch in transcendent sex begins to permeate all aspects of our existence, our Beingness begins to show up in our lives more often.

This Being-based experience results in us being more loving. Increased awareness and spontaneous insight can also arise, due to increased access to higher intelligences, and the inherent properties of Being. To say the least, this can open to satisfying life potentials, authentic transformation, and may support spiritual awakening. Mindful and, profound considerations do arise when sensing into whether such natural and truth-based approaches to sex and love are what you are in alignment with, and whether this is something you are drawn toward. Indeed, what is ultimately calling is a broader and more robust orientation, motivation, and reason to cultivate conscious sex and love with another.

It takes familiarity, and an artful sense of it all, to see that this is normal, and to have a desire to stabilize this Essential Presence together (and single or partnered, to be able access, radiate, and stabilize this as an individual). The very first time I experienced this aspect of existence with a partner was about 10 years after my daughter was born. Fortunately it was with someone who was as equally dedicated to understanding the mysteries of sexuality and spirituality, otherwise one can see how it may have been very disturbing! We had a moment when we were looking at each other, and realized that we were stabilized in the space of shared Essential Presence. It was not just a flash, and we could keep being with each other there, very directly. There was a startling vividness, and she playfully said to me, almost unable to get her words out without choking on her erupting laughter, with her eyes sparkling with some strange new truth, "Who the f--k are you? And how did we get here?" And, after a moment of deafening silence, her eyes glowing, we literally almost passed out from laughter; the joy, innocence, power, and robust connection was utterly, completely, and permanently life changing. This was a living love, which honestly, has no words. And the magnetism towards one another's sense of Being, and bodies– sexual yes, but man-oh-man, so much more than sexual, whoa. In some ways, with huge respect, in comparison, this "hi-gain" connection almost frames the sense of romantically being in love as a kind of entertainment, albeit a spectacular kind of entertainment–like watching a movie of a spectacular spot in nature instead of being there. This kind of connection is also a phenomenal resource if relationship challenges come up, which by-the-way, we found almost always originate from a lesser sense of self, or our ego, one might say. Rather than bypassing them, it truly puts conflict in a remarkable context. In fact, as an aside, from another direction, solid conflict resolution, often opens up ego.

Are we relating and having sex like this all the time? No, we are not but once we become familiar with relating, and being sexual like this, all levels of relating and being sexual improve, from a "quickie," to transcendent sex.

If coupled, of course this approach to sexual love has periods where the degree of attention a couple shares varies. Yet I have found, as these natural robust embodiments become integrated, a broad landscape of shared existence, rich with living texture and aliveness often emerges. Conflicts and misunderstandings tend to occur much less often. The sense of routine, or becoming a pattern or habit for one another, which is a challenge that many longer-term partners face and experience, tends to arise much less often.

Perhaps most importantly, shared Essential Presence empowers a couple in making the living decision to consciously stay together on an ongoing basis. Or, if it becomes apparent that a relationship is done, if partnering ends: to be as available as possible when releasing from partnering, to support separating in love, with compassion and mutual respect.

I can tell you first hand, consciously decoupling (a new term emerging for caring, conscious couples transitioning out of partnership) is an incredible experience. It is always hard to have a partnership come to close, but doing so consciously, while staying connected, is an empowering and life-giving gift to each partner, even when facing the loss and grief of a partnership ending. In my personal and professional life experience, I can say directly, that couples where at least one person is able to access Essential Presence are much more likely to be able to do so. If both partners are able to access and share Essential Presence, it is all the more likely. This directly alleviates one of life's greatest sources of fear. There is less fear because when there is a sense that you can access, and even share Essential Presence, then a powerful sort of trust in life arises. This trust, once experienced, is truly comforting. It is not trust from a place of security (a fear driven impulse sometimes in play to stay together), but trust which originates through a core trust in existence. All this resource, even in the face of difficulty, is a testimony to what can be available when accessing and sharing Essential Presence.

If you are single, familiarity with these competencies will contribute immeasurably to your confidence and charisma, and the quality of people you attract.

Whomsoever you attract and become involved with, will be much more aligned with your highest potential — this is a true secret to much better compatibility.

I have come to see in my work and in my own experiences, that even when we have really "done our work," sooner or later we come to see how our ego sense-of-self fundamentally limits, even co-opts, the experience of sexuality, and it often obscures the true nature of love.

If we step back for a moment and ponder this, it can be suddenly astounding to recognize how incredibly powerful and potent sex and sexuality is, and how mysterious, and even indefinable, love is. And yet, it is easy to go about life with widespread, but difficult to see, assumptions about sex and love that can significantly lessen our entire experiences of being in a sexual-love relationship.

I can say this with professional observation, and also intense personal experience, as mentioned earlier in this chapter, that very often, our egoic sense of self has its own interpretation of sex and love which blocks us from the actual experience of sex and love. This egoic interpretation can also result in our being in a relationship with an interpretation of our partner. In other words we can find ourselves being in a relationship with our interpretation of who we think that our partner is as person, which is not necessarily the truth of who that person really is. Think about this. It happens a lot. Until I was aware of this tendency, I was subject to it as well.

Hence, unexamined, we ultimately "define" sex, love, and even another... when these are indefinable.

When we are in relationship in this way, we can miss out on a whole lot of amazing sex and big love.

If we are truly interested in what is really going on inside an intimate relationship, we can begin to see just how valuable shared Essential Presence and expanded sexual skills can be. As we let go of our fascination with our interpretations of the sex, love, and the person we are intimate with, we can often thrive in the aliveness of how things actually are.

We begin to see how our consciousness works with reality, and how our consciousness works and dances with another's consciousness. We begin to see how such experience refines our consciousness. We also begin to see that as our consciousness becomes more refined, our present state of consciousness is the most important factor in determining what our future will look like. When our consciousness becomes more refined, our future opens to the higher consciousness that is wanting to come into this world today. When we become open to the higher consciousness that is coming into this world today, this becomes directly reflected in the quality we experience in our sexual-love relationships.

We can open to a direct experience of sex and love; one that is somewhat beyond words, but well within our capacity to know and experience; a body and Soul-opening ecstasy, a deep, deep love, and a living sense of connection.

The cultivation of shared Essential Presence and expanded sexual skills together in conscious love partnership, can induce profound experiences of intimacy, love, and connection, which do not dull with time, because they are infinite in nature. Such artful competency can also support spiritual awakening. For those with whom this resonates, we can call this a true re-enchantment, arousing us with the deeper power of sex and the mystery of love. The choices we make in how we experience sex, love, and partnering, to a very large extent, will determine how clearly we see and experience ourselves, our partner, and the true aliveness and richness of reality itself. Living with such clarity, we can truly draw deeply upon the powerful, erotic life energies embedded in sexuality, which keep us open, deeply fulfilled, and intrigued with the mysteries of love and existence. Get my bonus gift "Two Experiential Keys to Exploring Conscious Sexuality" here: http://blisslifepress.com/conscious-love/bonuses/.

The Power of Authentic Relating

Lucia Nicola Evans

"I see you.
May you know that you are deeply loved and guided. Take time to listen
and receive it.
Relax into this moment, you won't regret it.
To live an inspired life, follow your intuition
and be true to yourself.
Have as much fun as you can
without compromising yourself.
Surrender the bullshit and be at peace here and now.
Self-care is vital. Create time to give to yourself daily.
I am able to serve and love more people
when I am healthy.
Cuddle your way to wholeness.
The cure for depression is great love making.
Meditation is my Health Assurance. It keeps me centered and in touch who
I am.
The quality of your attention is important and is based on how present you
are.
I hear you with my soul.
The slower you go, the faster you get here."
Lucia Nicola Evans

We have lost our way as a species. We are expected to produce like machines. Our lives have become about making money and getting results, and figuring out how to survive. At a core level, our human psyche wants to feel safe. It wants to be loved and accepted for who it is, not just for what we do. Taking care of ourselves and loving ourselves is vital for our health and wellbeing. We thrive on reassurance and honest loving feedback from others. We feel a sense of belonging when we can relax and be ourselves, giving and receiving love in an authentic way. What makes Authentic Relating powerful is that it creates a safe space for us to share our thoughts, feelings and needs honestly with love and acceptance.

What makes Authentic Relating so Important?
Authentic Relating is important because it feeds our heart and soul. Without it, we start dying inside and the sparkle in our eyes begins to fade until there is no more light. Life without light becomes dull, monotonous and depressing. Authentic Relating also feeds our passion and purpose. It keeps us engaged with one another and connected to our true selves. It is an honest and real way of expressing ourselves that is beyond right and

wrong. As we share from our own truth, we become alive once again. The sparkle in our eyes becomes brighter and brighter and we live a rich and fulfilling life, with depth and true intimacy. Here we are connected to a state which is real, the truth of this moment. From here we feel free to be who we truly are, rather than feel the need to prove ourselves in order to feel loved and accepted.

Authentic Relating creates opportunities for us to grow and discover new ways of seeing things. We can use others as a mirror where we have the ability to see our blind spots more clearly. We then discover our insecurities and what needs healing, in order to restore love and acceptance. This way of relating gives us permission to be honest without feeling judged.

Sometimes being loving isn't enough to keep the sparkle alive in relationships. Honesty creates intimacy. There was no trust between me and one of my primary relationships. It had been broken on both sides. No matter how hard I tried, nothing seemed to work. The best thing I did was to get honest with myself, be grateful for what I learned and leave the relationship, realizing that nothing would resolve the issues. We just weren't compatible.

Why We Avoid Authentic Relating
Most of us avoid sharing what we really think and feel. We would rather be in control than venture out of our comfort zone for fear of being judged or rejected. So many of us get hurt and feel discouraged when we trust someone only to be let down by betrayal or mistrust. Over time, we tend to trust less and less. Being honest and sharing what we think and feel is often intimidating for this reason. Rarely do we have a safe place to share our true thoughts and feelings, a place where we can ask for what we need and be received and accepted unconditionally. It is easier to shut our hearts down and disconnect from others than to face the possibility of rejection or conflict.

Not sharing my thoughts and feelings wasn't an option for me. I tried not sharing for a period of time and my body rebelled. The energy started building in my body. Because I didn't know a healthy way to express myself, my body started attacking itself in the form of an auto-immune disease called Rheumatoid Arthritis. For my own health and wellbeing, I learned how to share my feelings and thoughts in a way that worked for me.

When I set a clear intention and let the person know what I want in a heartfelt way, I am often received with openness. I am not only able to share my feelings and thoughts; I am able to hold loving space for others to share their feelings and thoughts. I feel honored when others feel safe enough to share things with me they wouldn't usually share with others. It helps me to feel connected and safe.

One of the most Fundamental Components of Authentic Relating
Learning how to listen with compassion is key, not just learning how to listen with our ears. When we learn how to listen with our hearts, we create space for compassionate listening. Here we learn to listen behind the words and content, to the feelings, tonality and body language or physiology. Listening behind the words is helpful for us to deepen our understanding of each other where we gain more information about what is really going on, by tuning into the feelings and unmet needs. In order to be effective in our listening, we need to go beyond our experience and feel what it might be like for the other. This is where we can get a glimpse of how their world might be from their perspective.

At the age of one and a half, I lost my hearing in my left ear with a high fever, mild mumps and meningitis. I learned how to listen in other ways to compensate for my deafness. I watched the physiology of each person with depth and focused attention. I would notice how people transmitted their energy and connect to how they were feeling. I was fascinated why people did what they did. So I became an acute observer of people. I began to listen with my awareness.

In NLP, Neuro Linguistic Programming, they state that 7% of our communication are the words we use, 38% is how we say what we say, our tone, and 55% of our communication is our physiology. When we become masters at communication, listeners, speakers and observers, our armor is diminished and we feel safer to be our true self. We also feel acknowledged when someone deeply listens with their heart to what is painful. A key connector in authentic relating is acknowledgement, for it brings us into a receptive space because we feel recognized and important. From here, we are more willing to listen with an open heart. When there is space to listen, we feel received and seen. The next time you are in a conflict, external or internal, find something to acknowledge in that person or in yourself. Be specific and direct and notice what happens.

What does it mean to be Self Responsible and why is this important in Authentic Relating?

In order to have success in how we authentically relate, we need to become self-responsible. To become self-responsible, we need to develop awareness as to what words we use and how we say them, as well as in how we respond to people and life's circumstances. We can also greatly impact how others respond to us from our body language. People will intuitively know whether they can trust us or not. We need to become aware of our experience and how we treat ourselves and others around us. Learning self-respect is a core component of self-responsibility. Owning our stuff is vital. In order to own our stuff, we need to get to know ourselves in an intimate way. To really own our experience, 'I statements' are important. This creates a safe place to explore with love rather than making judgments that something should be different than it is. Another powerful way to be self-responsible is seeking to understand others first.

This diminishes reactivity and creates more room for true intimacy and connection, especially when there are differences.

At school I felt insecure. I believed I wasn't smart. I had every reason to believe this, since the feedback from my school and teachers showed me that I wasn't getting the information like everyone else. Later, I realized I just had a different way of learning and I wasn't acknowledged for it. My experience at school left me with low confidence. I quickly realized I had a choice. I could choose to shift from blaming the school for my low confidence level, and claim my power back. I have shown myself that I am very intelligent. Whatever I put my mind to, I've achieved.

Why is it Important to Know What Triggers us?
It is helpful to know our triggers and what shuts our hearts down so we can be more prepared when it happens. Our triggers tell us about our wounding and where we don't feel good enough. When we are triggered, it is often because we didn't get certain needs met in the past. To protect ourselves, we react, and our systems go into 'fight or flight' mode. We then make stories that we attach meanings to, to justify our position. Because of our wounding, we each have things to overcome and heal as we discover our truth. This makes Authentic Relating a very important part of our growth and success. Noticing when we react and take things personally is a practice unto itself. Most of us take things personally and don't know an alternative way. Our hearts close and we shut down. We feel alone and miserable inside. We become stuck and isolate ourselves from fear of potential hurt.

One of my triggers is abandonment. One day, I was having a conversation with my partner, and he was talking about working abroad for six months. He mentioned in the same breath that I could stay home and take care of things. Because I love him so much, this brought up my trigger of feeling abandoned. Because I was aware of my trigger, I was able to speak in a calm voice and let him know I was triggered. I was able to let him know I needed time to work through my feelings. I went in my own space, felt the feelings, and was then available to share with my partner what happened in a calm non-blaming voice.

Not everyone has developed the awareness to do this, and when we are triggered it is usually hard to talk in a loving voice. It is helpful to have a plan of action as to how to deal with triggers, especially in partnership before the trigger happens. This will enable each person to respect the other when they are triggered, knowing that they will eventually come back together and talk about what happened once the trigger subsides. This creates a deeper trust and respect for each individual's process. It may take 10 minutes, 30 minutes or days for the trigger to be worked through. Alone time is necessary for the individuals involved so that they can feel and reflect on the event that activated the trigger, enabling the triggers to subside. We need to notice our attitude. Are we blaming others or are we able to see our behavior for what it is where we come from a place of owning our healing, taking responsibility for our own triggers and being grateful for the lessons they give us?

Triggers are an important component of personal growth. They help us see where we still need to grow ourselves in order to be the best self we can be. Some of the most common triggers are feeling jealous, comparing ourselves with others where we don't feel good enough, not feeling accepted or respected for who we are, not being listened to, being wrongly accused and judged and of course there is the typical arguing and shouting matches that often escalate to anger, frustration and resentment.

The way to move past the trigger is first to acknowledge that you are triggered and that it is your responsibility to make time to move through your trigger. You must take time to stop and breathe and slow down to identify what the trigger is and what story you are telling yourself. It is important to take time to reflect and become aware of what you are feeling and where you are feeling the trigger in your body. The trigger is resolved when the charge is gone. You will know the charge is gone when there is no need to defend, attack or justify your position. Inquiring what the message is around the wounding is helpful for deep lasting results.

Only after you create space from the trigger with awareness, compassion and understanding, can you have the power to choose to relate from a place of love restoring harmony in your relationships.

The Importance of Knowing Our Values
Our values are a key ingredient in Authentic Relating. When we are clear as to what is important to us, we can clearly discern our priorities. Knowing our values affects our daily choices and how we manage our time and attention. We have a stronger sense of purpose when we consciously choose who we want to spent time with and why. As we become more aware and discerning where we put our attention, we have more ability to have a positive lasting impact on others, while sustaining our own inspiration and connection with what feels true to us.

One of my values is being present. It is important to me to be present when I relate with others. The more present I am, the deeper my understanding is, and the more opportunity I have at bringing harmony and inspiration to how I relate.

When I am upset, I want someone who is present to be with me. This is such a gift to offer presence to each other. Experiment next time, just being present with someone, letting go of the need to say anything, or fix anything or even to do anything. Just be present with an open heart, and notice what happens.

One of my dear soul sisters, Opal Love, used presence and seeing her friend for who she truly was to overcome a major conflict. She was in conflict with a woman, Ally, with whom she was living at the time. Opal felt in competition with Ally. They were avoiding sharing their truth with each other, because it was so uncomfortable. Finally, the tension was too much for them to bear. Ally initiated the conversation and suggested that they go to see a shaman to restore their friendship. The shaman had them gaze into each other's eyes without words, just being present with one another. Then after a few minutes they shared a few words of acknowledgment which brought them back to harmony.

In this story, friendship was more valuable than being in competition with each other. Notice, it did take one of them to initiate a shift and then a willingness for the other to agree to go see the shaman.

In heated moments, resentment, frustration and anger builds. With Authentic Relating, emotional build-up gets cleared away and resolved. It was amidst the height of Opal's feelings of anger and frustration with Ally that she equally found strength in her faith with love. The only way out of her conflict was through it. She saw the true value only after her experience with Ally. Opal saw the benefit of having direct honest communication, even when fear was present. Her truth was the essence that was needed to sustain and restore a heart connection between herself and Ally. She was able to be a reflection, and help her see and feel her own truth. Opal said, "When I allowed my authentic self to be seen, Ally could see me for who I truly was and I could see her for who she truly was."

This conflict was transformational for both Opal and Ally. Because they were able to work through it, their relationship is much stronger.

The Gift of Feelings
One of my favorite people, Maya Angelou said, "I've learned that people will forget what you said, people will forget what you did, but people will never forget how you made them feel."

Having courage to feel our feelings and share what is vulnerable, brings us into alignment with our hearts. We also feel more tender and open, giving us the opportunity to experience deeper intimacy. When we are honest with our feelings and express our truth regularly, we gain self-confidence, especially when we are not looking for external approval. We need willingness and courage to step out of our comfort zones and create the time and space for Authentic Relating. It is only when we get brutally honest with ourselves, and have the willingness to move into the resistance, that we have the opportunity to create new experiences in our relationships.

I often thought it was a sign of strength if I didn't cry. When I was a little girl, I was taught to 'pull myself together' and not to cry. It may have seemed like a sign of strength, yet I soon realized that I was not being true to myself. I discovered it was okay to be vulnerable, and that having the courage to feel my feelings, was a true sign of strength and power.

I have changed and overcome much turmoil and tremendous suffering and misunderstanding in my life. I have discovered ways of relating that feel most authentic, true and natural to me. I feel I am honoring and respecting myself the most, when I am being with my feelings. Being with my feelings is natural, yet it felt very awkward for the longest time. I didn't feel at ease relating to others. I wanted to feel safe to be myself, but because I didn't feel as though I measured up to certain standards or expectations in the world, I didn't feel good enough. I didn't feel safe to be me. This created a sense of lack of self-worth, and a lack of confidence. I felt lost and trapped in my own body. I got depressed. I had high anxiety about living in the world. Because I didn't know how to accept myself for who I was, I felt deeply rejected and alone. Many people resort to suicide, head to the mental hospital, or take anti-depressants when they feel this way. Suicide and medication were not options for me, so I chose various natural healing modalities, one of which was Authentic Relating. I slowly created enough safety for myself, and created authentic relationships in community, as well as, becoming more self-aware. This shifted my desire to leave this planet. I was here to stay, for I felt safe to be in my own skin, finally knowing how to feel my feelings.

How Loving Touch Helped Me Feel Safe to Express Myself
Not only did I receive massage, I practiced massage for nine years. I felt so connected to people through touch. For a long time, touch was the only way I felt safe to relate with others. Not only did touch help me feel safe to feel my feelings, but touch and massage helped me to feel safe to be intimate with others. Because I felt an instant connection that was beyond words, I could relax. It was powerful to know I could make people feel safe, with just my touch. Touching with clear loving intention, not only helped me relax, it helped others relax enough to connect with their feelings and to learn how to feel them. My touch brought people into their hearts and made them more aware of their bodies. This was refreshing to me. Touch cut through the small talk, and went right into the core of what was real, quickly reminding us to return to the moment and to share authentically.

Where and With Whom Can Authentic Relating Be Practiced?
Authentic Relating can be practiced anywhere. It is more supportive to do it in a private, quiet space. We can practice Authentic Relating with ourselves, in partnership with our lovers, in family dynamics, in community and with our business partners, as well. Authentic Relating is for you if you want to feel safe, and if you desire to be in a space where you can be totally honest about what you feel and think, while being received unconditionally, without judgment.

My Invitation to You to Become More Aware in How You Relate with Yourself and Others

Start to become curious about what drives your behavior and why. What makes you mad and why? Notice how you feel. What are some of your needs, and what are they fulfilling?

Create space in your day, and slow down enough to feel your feelings. What wisdom are they showing you? Make time to breathe, to release the tension, and allow yourself to become receptive to your truth. What is your experience when you wake up? How do you start your day? What are you saying to yourself? Do you start your day with an attitude of gratitude, or do you say, "oh... not another day at work... I hate work!"?

What is your experience in your life? Are you living in fear, or are you taking risks and living full out? How can you become more receptive to Authentic Relating? What will you receive as a result of creating space and time for Authentic Relating? What will you be able to do when you feel safe to express yourself authentically— beyond criticism, where you are truly accepted for who you are?

I See You: A Message from My Heart to Yours, Giving You a Taste of the Power of Authentic Relating
Serving the Divine, as a beacon of light, I have been sent to Planet Earth to be your Spirit Guide. I am here to guide you to live from your true self. Know you are so loved. You are so powerful. You have the ability to choose how you want to relate in each moment. You are a refined musical instrument. Bringing more awareness to your blind spots will help you operate your instrument with refinement and precision. In order to get the results you want in your relationships, awareness is key for you to resonate with your truth, your unique vibration. You see, everything is made up of different vibrations, and each vibration is a specific frequency of energy. Your words and how you speak affect the people around you and how they respond to you. Your words are very powerful and often have a lasting impact that you don't often see or know about.

I love you so much, Precious Heart. I see who you are. I see into your soul. If you are hiding, it is your time to come out. There is no need to hide any longer. It is safe to come out. I am here to remind you that you are empowered to feel supported, loved and free. For it is not until you free yourself from the identification of your limited thinking, belief systems, and trauma, that you can feel at peace within. Once you are at peace, you can co-create, play, live in harmony, joy and love as you evolve living as your true self.

I appreciate you so much. Thank you for picking up this book. Selecting this book tells me a lot about you. It tells me that you are interested in learning how to love and become more conscious in how you relate with yourself and others. Thank you for this. The truth is you are extremely important to this planet at this time. The fact is, the world would be different if you were not here. It would vibrate differently. Yes, you are so powerful that you have an effect on the entire planet by your very existence. You are more important to this journey called life than you can ever imagine.

Just by you being here, in this world, in a body, inspires me. I am so grateful you chose to be born. Thank you. Your reflection helps me feel myself again, and helps me remember who I am. Thank you for being alive. Your presence gives me a purpose to live. I get to love and share and play WITH you as you show up more and more.

I want you to feel like royalty, because you are. I want you to feel honored like you have never felt honored before. I ACCEPT you fully as you are, right here, right now. My wish for you, after reading this chapter, is that you will have an experience of yourself that will help you feel the power of your own authenticity. By being authentic, loving and gentle with yourself, you will have a deeper clarity and experience of yourself and with anyone who comes into your field of awareness. With clarity and direct experience comes access to true power.

Know that I really SEE you. I see you through my knowingness. I see your true magnificence and beauty. You are radiant love packed in an incredible package called 'your body', with the message 'VERY FRAGILE' written on it.

You have been called here to planet Earth to remember and embody your true self— who you already are. To remember yourself as pure radiant love underneath all the 'bubble wrap' that surrounds your inner being. The 'bubble wrap' represents your fears and insecurities that have accumulated during your years on this planet. Your fears and insecurities prevent the love from flowing in and out.

Listen for love. I dare you to live full out. Love completely. Live as if life is a journey of self-discovery, discovering along the way what works and what doesn't. Allow time and space for Authentic Relating. Let go of the programming, and be aware as you unravel the societal programming, your fears and insecurities. Remember to live your truth, opening your heart wider and wider each day, where you honor yourself in every way.

Just imagine for a moment— Imagine loving yourself fully and, by loving yourself fully, you feel whole and complete. From your wholeness you have the ability to love others fully in their wholeness, with total acceptance. Imagine how much freedom you would feel, and how much peace and joy you would experience. Imagine not holding back your love. Imagine not feeling the need to be dependent on others to be happy, joyful and loving. Imagine a life where you know how to share love with reverence and honor, and how to be and receive love with the total acceptance of each moment. What would this feel like to you? Can you imagine this as being possible? What do you need to change or let go of in yourself for this to be possible?

I want to invite you to take a journey of self-discovery with me, where you will be able to explore how to let go of insecurity having power over you, where you make friends with all of your insecurities, and live as your true self, where each moment of your life is aligned with what is true for you. Promise yourself something right now. Promise that you will always be true to yourself. For when you are true to yourself, you have more love to offer those around you. Thank you for your courage and your willingness to learn and grow. Thank you.

Because I value you so much, I want to offer you a special gift. I know you will love it. I have two surprises you will find will bring magic to your life. Click on this link to discover what they are. http://blisslifepress.com/conscious-love/bonuses/

In Summary

The more we practice Authentic Relating, the more permission we give ourselves to be true in each moment. This brings an element of freedom and relief to our existence. We can finally relax and be ourselves without the need for pretense in order to impress or feel accepted. Self-sabotage, protecting our hearts, and not trusting become experiences of the past. Over time, we learn to become compassionate and aware with ourselves when self-sabotage creeps in, or misunderstanding takes ahold, and we feel the need to defend, attack, or criticize.

What gives us freedom in how we relate with ourselves and each other, is the ability to choose how we respond in each moment. Choosing how we respond gives us time and space to drop into our hearts. When we drop into our hearts, by taking time to pause and breathe, we create space to choose how we want to respond. In reacting we lose our power to choose with love. This puts us at the mercy of reaction and fear, taking us into self-protection, shutting our hearts down and creating disconnection.

When we practice Authentic Relating on a regular basis to express our truth, the way we talk with ourselves and each other begins to change. We begin to soften how we say things and to have more patience. We feel more empowered, as we bring awareness and love into how we relate. We begin to see our true selves, and really see one another for who we really are, leaving us with a deep sense of acceptance and inner peace. Just by making time to practice Authentic Relating, we become more loving and conscious, leaving us with deeper, richer, more connected and fulfilling relationships.

From here, we can begin to co-create deeper intimacy with honesty and openness. Now we have created deep trust. From here we can build a new world that is in alignment with our true nature. We then have the ability to live in harmony, where we have much more opportunity to have fun, sharing ourselves with each other without fear or judgement. Living together in truth, peace and love is the way of true Authentic Relating.

Staying True to Your Own Heart
Moving on from love that didn't work out

Kristina Shumilova

"Love doesn't offer guarantee, and it isn't always fair, or gentle. And that's
not going to change. Break-ups shake things up.
And to move on from love that didn't work out what needs to change is
the way we go about it. Instead of making it a passive isolating process,
take an
opportunity to make it an empowering one. It is a process that's natural,
and allows you to reconnect with who you truly are. It doesn't break you,
it builds you up."
Kristina Shumilova

About six years ago, I was really starting to question my life. Everything
seemed fine on the surface, but underneath, I was unbearably restless.

Our 5th anniversary was coming up, and my husband and I continued
drifting apart, becoming more like friends or even roommates who didn't
even like spending time together anymore. I didn't talk to people about
this because I was supposed to be happy. It took a long time to become
aware of how much time I was spending throwing 'nobody understands
me' pity parties. I was stuck in circular logic. The same thoughts were
always running around in my mind. "Maybe this is how life is when you
grow up," I thought. I didn't like that idea, but I wanted to know why my
heart was breaking over and over again.

My husband and I used to be happy, and I didn't want anyone to know
that now we weren't. I began to judge myself, and was constantly getting
irritated with him. I saw things from my parents' relationship that were
being recreated in my own marriage, and that angered me even more.

There was a moment when my husband asked me a question about where
I saw myself in five years. My mind blanked. I don't know exactly what I
saw, but I knew he wasn't there with me. He wasn't in my future five
years from now, and it hurt because I still couldn't bring myself to think of
life without him, and I certainly wasn't ready to make the move.

I had two big reasons that were holding me back from leaving. One, I was
worried that I couldn't figure out my life without him, and being alone was
scary. Two, I believed I was a bad person if I left him when he wasn't
feeling strong about himself.

I was exhausted by the constrictions I felt that were living within me. There was a growing hunger within for spontaneity, laughter and adventure. I yearned for romance and space to move around in. I could no longer ignore the urge for freedom... my freedom, a freedom I was born with and had chosen to deny.

The next year and a half was long, as I invested most of my energy in trying to make our relationship work and scrutinizing myself. It's hard to admit. When I finally brought up the conversation about our marriage, he said it had been weighing heavily on his mind, too. He shared that he couldn't bring himself up to talk about it either. Even though it hurt for both of us, we mutually decided to give our marriage a break.

I didn't know what I was going to do, but I knew I was done doing what I didn't want to do anymore. I cried, and smoked cigarettes. Deep inside I knew this was exactly what needed to happen. And still, I smoked more. It wasn't easy, but I knew I could no longer be this woman who couldn't be fully honest, was feeling disconnected from herself and others, and was living a half-life.

Perhaps you can relate to my story, nodding your head, as I share my intimate feelings. This is why I created this chapter, to show you how to be your own heart's expert. I share the mental, emotional, and sometimes even the imaginary phases of letting go of the past, while staying true to your heart. And because I believe less is more, I am going to keep it simple.

I am not here to give you love or dating advice. I am here as a guide to help you open up without having to defend myself. You can be a hero or heroine that doesn't give up or give in, and stays true to their heart.

I promise not to copy-paste my own dreams and values onto your life.

To start, let's be clear; this isn't about 'him' or' her'. It is not about that whole story in the past. When love doesn't work out, one can easily start to slip down into the self-doubt. The slippery slope is where you tell yourself 'I am not good enough' or 'this is too much'. My vision for you is to be your own heart's expert. The one that's alive, and not perfect, yet beautiful in your own way.

It took me a couple of weeks to get myself together and even to break the news to my family in Siberia, Russia. I waited because I didn't want to worry them. Also, I wasn't raised in a family where being emotional was okay. I grew up to be really good at hiding my feelings. The only time I expressed my feelings was with friends. It took me awhile to turn that around, to share, and just be myself. It was a lot of inner work to be able to not follow what people wanted me to be. Life still reminds me to do that in new and different ways, if I ever find myself believing into the old stories.

When I finally shared the news of the breakup, my mother reacted in fear. "You have nobody there now! Come home!" I know she cares, but all I could hear in her voice then was fear. This was the last thing I needed and wanted to hear all the way on the other side of the planet.

A few months later I went to visit my family, and had a sort of heart to heart with my mother about my life, and why things didn't work out. I remember telling her, "I am tired of always having to be strong. I want to be with someone I can allow myself to be weak with, and still feel supported."

Even though she had had to become a strong woman in her own life, she looked at me and said, "But you are who you are," as if this is something I am supposedly stuck with.

I then realized who "I am" is going to have to change. I knew I couldn't grow from that perspective. I also didn't want my life to be built from fear, and lack. This inner choice meant, for now, I was on my own.

Despite my parents, or perhaps because of them, I went back to the US to recreate my life from my own heart. I was done living by anyone else's ideas of what is possible. Choosing, daily, my own vision over the old stories was the key; stepping outside of the noise and into the quiet of who I am became my life.

I was no longer willing to buy into the old stories. I now truly knew that the only person that could hold me back was myself. This was not easy, but so worth it.

New friendships and people started to flow into my life. I was genuinely starting to feel happy. I was living my life forward. I was loving myself, my choices and my life.

And then he walked into my life; the man of my dreams. Love is hard to put into words, but if I had to I would say I've never felt connected in such a beautiful and awakened way in my entire life. For the first time ever I, instinctively, intuitively, and wholeheartedly, felt like I could even have a child with this man.

Not too long after, I discovered there was another woman in this picture. One can easily take sides in these moments, and begin to think it is 'him', and question this man's integrity.

I could have slammed the door in his face, harbored anger and walked away with it.

What happened next changed me in a very surprising way. Instead of walking away and keeping my feelings to myself, I allowed myself to start crying in front of him. At first it felt as if I was falling apart in front of him, and that was wrong. But the beauty was, I was no longer willing to not express how I truly felt. I was no longer willing to pretend to be someone else. I felt a belief in myself, and a knowing it wasn't about him. It was about me. This is a powerful realization to embody.

Here is What I Have to Say to That Younger Me:
"Yes, you felt connected as you never had before. Isn't that beautiful? You are lucky, and so is he. Value your experiences. You are no ordinary girl. This will deeply transform you. You'll be glad one day. Invest yourself in the things that awaken you into being who you truly are, growing and shining love and light into every corner of your imperfections. Your story will inspire others to live up to their own visions. And always remember you have an important vision too. You are on the right path. I am so glad you won't settle for less."

I include this because one major problem I see in my work is how many people run up against a wall of self-doubt when they meet "the one". They go searching, hoping and waiting, and the moment arrives and the fear and doubt get in the way. Please be prepared, and then walk through that doubt into the arms of the "one".

Here are the three keys I learned from my experience that I wish for you to consider on your own journey:
1. Be YOU no matter what past discouragements exist.
2. The power to heal comes from within.
3. Love yourself first.

Be YOU no matter what happened in the past.
Be YOU no matter what happened in the past to discourage you. We all judge ourselves for our past, second-guessing the choices we made, thinking we made mistakes by opening our hearts. We feel because we allowed someone into our world, and it didn't work out as hoped, that we somehow let them take from us.

Here is an important key to being your own heart's expert and living a life of self-love and freedom: life will continue challenging you. It has nothing to do with you being wrong, or making mistakes; it is part of life. There is no reason to pretend to be perfect at it. Be yourself. You can't conquer love by trying to fix yourself. You don't attract the "one" because your skin is perfect, or your thighs are just the right size or shape. You attract, give and enjoy love because you are being love to yourself. Deep inside you know not to give up on who you truly are. Work on the inner you and connect to the light that glows from the center of your heart. Then you will be able to share, and receive love exactly as you are and exactly as you like it.

The Power to Heal Comes from Within.

The power to heal comes from within. The process of letting go comes from your whole being, from your own center. It is strangely liberating to let go, even if it feels painful in the moment. Instead of feeling as if you are trying to glue broken pieces back together, let the power to heal come from within you and become whole through self-acceptance.

If there is one thing I've learned it's to grow from your experiences without giving in or giving up on yourself. Build your life forward, not by dragging the past with you. Moving on is beyond just "talking about it" or "taking advice". Move beyond the expectation of "having moved on already", and beyond trying to "think" your way through it with your logical and analytical mind.

Heal yourself by letting go of any worry that you may never love again. Release the belief that you may never heal from your past relationships, and may never get over it and love again. Find that place inside of you that lives and breathes this power to heal, and without trying to understand it intellectually, let it move, and expand inside. Stop the worrying; it is like paying interest on a loan you may never get.

Love Yourself First
Love yourself first no matter what your relationship status is. EVER. Wondering how do you actually do that? Well, there is no cookie cutter formula, and it's different for everyone. I believe it's simple. For me, loving myself means believing in myself. For someone else it could mean taking good care of their body. For others loving themselves means maintaining a spiritual practice that's keeping their heart and soul in tune with their desires and dreams. To find an answer to what loving yourself means for you, ask yourself these questions:
1. How do you know when you are not loving yourself?
2. What needs to change to love and accept yourself?
3. What does it mean for you "Love yourself first"?

Give it a thought, and greet what arrives from your deep knowing.

The reason I shared my story transparently, is so you know you don't have to be perfect. You don't have to feel broken, alone and unworthy. Stop being so hard on yourself for making a mistake or two; they will turn out to not be mistakes in the end anyway. I am curious about the depth of your true nature; I'm not interested in the superficial. I see you, as you are, and I honor you on your journey.

This is an invitation to give up giving up and reconnect to your true nature of love.

I am inviting you to be your most curious self here, and open up to the possibility that moving on from love that didn't work out doesn't have to be a passive, isolating process. Instead it can be an empowering and awakening experience that doesn't break you but actually builds you up.

You are on the right path.

Most people have at least one love story to tell. I am sure you do too, unless you never became curious about what it feels like to kiss; to look another human in the eyes without any pretense; to hold hands, and feel like anything is possible. Yet many of us found out that love isn't always gentle or fair. A lot of times it's beyond frustrating.

Because I understood the need for a different approach when it came to moving on, I created an approach that is dedicated to letting go in a positive and empowering way, so you can move into staying true to your own heart. I know going through a break-up, or moving on from love that didn't work out can be very hard. What saddens me most is that we close off our hearts to love because sometime, somewhere in the past someone happened to act meanly, carelessly... or worse, we thought they were "the one".

Have you ever felt a little stuck? Felt you want to let go, move on, and heal but you don't know how, so you try to keep busy with life yet feel deeply alone in it? You are not alone. Maybe you are having a hard time believing it is ever possible to find that special connection again or feel so discouraged by your experiences that you bought into some form of "I am not worthy of love".

Decide to become the caretaker of your own heart. It doesn't matter how much struggle you have experienced with love; you can begin to trust yourself and know you have the answers. Whether you are fresh out of a relationship or it may have been a while ago, if you are still feeling you failed that person, if you are judging yourself for not doing enough or being enough, now is the time to stop. Even if your last relationship wasn't really good for you, and there is still a cloud of negativity hanging over that story, you can free yourself from the heaviness and lighten up. Maybe it's the opposite, and you felt really connected to that person, and trying to date now just feels uninspiring. Stay to the path of loving self first, and the love will follow.

Often, after one or more breakups it can feel as if you live inside of the pattern of events, thinking over and over, and not trusting people, and wonder if it's ever possible for things to be different again. You might even feel no one truly understands what you are going through, and you are just stuck in it by yourself. I know it hasn't been easy. But I am here to tell you to trust you have the answer.

Take a moment to really look deep within and ask "What's really happening for me right now?"

Then think; if your mind were a library, what kind of books do you have in there? What do the kinds of books in your mind library reveal about how you are seeing life? Do the titles read 'Life is beautiful'? '5 Ways to Fall and

Stay in Love'? Or... do they read 'Top 10 Reasons Not to Open Up Your Heart'...?Explore this library in your heart and mind, and be curious about the stories you've been telling yourself.

Radical Responsibility
This process will heal and reconnect you to love, and it takes radical responsibility, honesty and vulnerability. Chances are, you've spent a lot of time thinking about things you don't want any more of; things you are done with, but keep thinking of. Things you'd never want to do again. It's common, so it's okay if you feel some resistance. Take a deep breath here, and let that resistance go. Now sit down to journal and let it pour out; do not interrupt the flow.

Important: you might be thinking that those thoughts are keeping you stuck, but they are actually driving you. They are driving your choices, even the way you've been feeling. So you can either choose to stay in the passenger seat without acknowledging who is driving and where they are taking you or you can find the courage to get behind that steering wheel and recreate your future. Celebrate life without the old stories.

I believe every relationship that doesn't work out is an opportunity to reconnect with yourself.

Wander into Your Life's Future Fantasy
Another key to this process is to realize you must explore: "Who would I be without those thoughts?" If they one day disappeared and you were unable to think from that place anymore.

• What would that feel like?
• Look like?
• Imagine yourself going about your day—free from those feelings.
• How would it feel talking with others?
• How would you react to opportunities that come your way?
• What's that like, being with yourself?
• How will it feel when you try on being the version of you who is free from those things you've been holding on to?

The time is right. I do believe that everything big starts with something small, and that by reading this chapter you will get curious about letting go of those worries and mistakes connected to your past. I invite you to wander into your life's future fantasy, and see a possibility for a new relationship.

Nourish your dreamer. Don't ever change to be loved. Change to love yourself first.

What is your vision, my hero or heroine? And are you ready to let go of the past without making it a struggle?

I believe love starts with you, and to support you on your journey I'd love to gift you Part 1 of my Virtual Heart and Soul Series created for you to move on, and let go of the past with ease.

I'll walk you through the process to release what's been holding YOU back. All you need for this is a cozy place you can just relax, and tune in. This series was created for women, but if you are a man I encourage you to listen in. I strongly believe you'll get as much out of it. Ready to get invited into your future without the old stories? Ready to celebrate love and life? You can access your gift here http://blisslifepress.com/conscious-love/bonuses/. From my heart to yours... love yourself first.

The Dance Of Love

Deborah Nielsen

"Why would we want to fall in love? Sounds like we might fall down, and lose our balance, or lose ourselves. We may fall in love, in an out of balance way,
when we are not taking care of ourselves, and get side tracked or escape from our core truth. The alternative is to start with our own self-love and balance, so that we can be in love.
Being in love does not have to be at the expense of our wholeness, but can develop as an extension of our core, resonating with a partner, through chemistry and with core character. Then we are able to grow in love instead of fall in love! Creating sustainable, collaborative partnership is possible.
We can dance together in the Dance of Love. The Dance of Life begins with our heartbeat and the natural rhythm within us.
We can be at home in our heart, and resonate from our heart.
Our insight and intuition can be our guiding compass. We can cultivate compassion and passion.
We can become more free to be ourselves, and enjoy the Dance of Life and the Dance of Love."
Deborah Nielsen

The beginning of life starts with dance.

When we are in utero, we are swaying and swimming and hearing the beat of the heart and the swoosh of body fluids. Before other senses develop, we are hearing and moving.

We are being held, and we are connected. And yet, we are separate.

We may think of it as our first music, and our first dance.

As babies, we are rocked, and once we start moving around, we may begin to develop our own forms of dance. This may be our second dance.

At the heart of it, love matters. From our first breath to our last breath, the loving bonds in our life give us hope, connection and meaning.

In relationship, from our first bond, there is the dance of togetherness and separateness. Dancing between and overlapping togetherness and separateness, is the dance of relationship.

Dance is a metaphor for love and relationship!

Part of a healthy, conscious relationship, is balancing togetherness and separateness, and honing our abilities to navigate the balance of being ourselves, and being in partnership. This is a dance, to be able move smoothly, with grace between our own domain and our love domain of partnership. One way to explore and expand the practice of conscious relationship is to look at and consciously practice compassion and insight. Practicing compassion and insight, we can more fully integrate and deepen our heart and mind, and develop greater contentment, resilience and sustainability in our relationships.

Insight springs from and nurtures our individuality. Insight can guide us in setting our boundaries, preferences, and being able to communicate on a deeper level. Babies coo, and cry and smile. Before verbal language, there is communication. We communicate by sound, scent, touch, and sight. We are gathering information by listening with our senses. To have a sense of self and a sense of safety, we need to be aware of our own bodies, hearts, minds, and spirit. We also need to be seen and heard. Healthy boundaries allow us to be able to know where we begin, and where we end, to help us to be aware of who we are.

As we pay attention to our intuition, listening to our gut, our heart, and other signals in our body, trusting this valuable information, our choices and actions are guided. We are empowered to discern what feels right in our heart of hearts. When we have the clarity to be able to make choices and to find our own rhythm, we can find our way. If we become overwhelmed with too much input, and there is too much chatter inside our heads, or from outside of ourselves via other people and/or media around us, we can lose touch with our own internal compass. Attuning with our internal compass can help us find our true path, and resonate with our integrity. Applying this compass of insight and intuition can assist us in connecting and integrating body, mind, heart, and spirit. If we are caught up in an addictive pattern, we lose touch with this compass, and our signals get crossed. When we put our attention and energy into a behavior pattern that is imbalanced, believing it will get us what we need, it is like hitting our head against the wall. There is no room for contentment here and no peace. Having some quiet time each day to clear our mind can help us align with our inner compass. This may, for example, be a walk in nature, or a time of prayer or meditation.

As we quiet the chatter in our minds, we have an opportunity to develop greater mental clarity and more peace in our hearts. Compassion is a form of love that nurtures inner kindness. Through compassion, we can find ourselves in a more accepting stance. We are not looking down with superiority or with sympathy. We are not looking up with envy or giving our power away. We are seeing and hearing from a place of equanimity. We can recognize our wholeness, being present with our whole self, body, heart, mind and spirit, and resonate this wholeness from our core. When we do this, we are in a clearer place to be present with another. Compassion can assist us on the path of building more present connection, and resonance, in the practice of being seen and heard, and in finding attunement. The practice of self-compassion is a way to connect with ourselves and nurture inner kindness.

Having outlets that involve movement and creativity can help us to tune in to our core center, bringing us back to our balance. There can be a dynamic balance, a dance that interweaves and flows between compassion and insight, and between togetherness and separateness.

If we fall in to fear or the need to control, we might tense up and are not able to dance in a fluid way. As we relax into the dance, staying aware and grounded in our body, we are able to feel more joy in the movement.

Being in a loving state, we may feel alive and confident, safe and free. Trust is a delicate fabric that is woven, in the dance of love, with honesty and respectful in caring communication. It is difficult to repair if torn. Safety is a vital foundation for love, trust, and sustainability. We can build love and trust with compassion and insight. We are able to navigate through obstacles and rough spots, as we have compassion with ourselves in setting boundaries. We can use our insight to discern our choices and where to invest our time and energy. With compassion and insight, we are in a better position to navigate our way through pain, distress and imbalance, and we are in a position to continue to grow with love and constructive communication. When we have a solid foundation of trust and love, we have the possibility of creating a sustainable, devotional relationship with the dance of love. In this dance of love, there can be harmony, and grace, and fluid interaction. In the dance of love, there is comfortable movement between togetherness and separateness.

As children, growing through stages of development there is a dance of togetherness and separateness. As babies, it is vital that we are held. Children need space to be themselves as well as a nurturing connection and clear communication and boundaries. As teenagers and young adults, we must make our own choices and have room to make mistakes. Along the way, as children, there is a dance between our independence and dependence. Children instinctively know how to be themselves. Children do well when they can express themselves creatively and be connected with nature. Ideally, as children grow, they feel secure with a parent bond, have time in nature, and are free to express themselves; knowing they can be seen, heard, cared for and protected. Throughout development, we navigate between the need to be our own person, and the need to be connected and to rely on others. I experienced raising my sons as a devotional practice of love. Parenting can be a dance of love.

In terms of communication and connection, there are parallels with parenting and partnering. We navigate and create a new dance in partnership, in the rhythm of togetherness and separateness. Growing up, we require the containment of home, and nourishment, and limits for safety, and we need the room to make choices and experiment so that we can learn about ourselves, others and our environment. We develop confidence by feeling good about our actions and decisions, and by an occasional fall that we bounce back up from.

Children know how to play, explore and create, as long as they are safe to do so. We can explore, play, learn and experiment. By raising children with a practice of conscious loving compassion, and by giving them the space and confidence to develop their own intuition and insight, we can strengthen their developmental foundation. This is all a practice, and there is no perfect way. As adults, we can continue to raise ourselves in some ways! Focusing on ideas of how a child should be, rather than accepting them as they are, can make it difficult for children to trust themselves. When we place a pre-constructed blueprint of how our partners should be, we could miss their true essence. Children do need space to be themselves and the emotional stability of healthy, respectful communication. Children need to know they are loved unconditionally, and that they are responsible for their behavior. Children are natural artists. When we are young, we paint and dance and sing without the idea of perfection or performance, but for the sheer joy and exploration of the process. This is the early dance, we may return to in order to tune into our own rhythm. This is the dance where we can learn how to love and accept ourselves, being absorbed in the process of dancing and connecting. Remembering or rediscovering our innocent, child self, is a part of being able to be playful and to develop our natural passion for life. Returning to this natural dance, we may have to unravel pain and patterns of behavior that are blocking us or tripping us up, rather than letting us be free to dance and connect in a natural, authentic way. Raising children with conscious compassion and insight helps to provide a strong developmental foundation. Some of us were given elements of this; for others there has been wavering attachment and support, which makes it more challenging to be at home with ourselves and secure in relationships. I believe we can all benefit by doing our own healing work and preventative practices of self-care, and immersing ourselves, when we are ready, in conscious, intentional, loving relationship. Heart heals heart. We can assist in healing each other with love and kindness.

With these elements, and mutual respect, flexibility, and clear expectations, children have the opportunity to feel confident and secure. This gives them the opportunity to become attuned to their own developing compass of insight. With the sense of safety on both a physical and emotional level, children are able to feel confident to play, learn and grow.

Love is humbling because there is always more to learn about ourselves and others. I struggle with humility at times. My temperament is partly fiery and willful. Getting out of my head and holding compassion for myself and others helps me to stay balanced. Humility is useful for keeping us from separating ourselves and falling into judgement, fear or criticism. This kind of train of thought throws us off track. Humility and compassion allows us to get out of ourselves and connect more with others, in an authentic way.

We all experience forms of suffering. The mind and body get triggered, and we experience a sense of danger. This can be intrusive. It can be a tremendous challenge to navigate our way through it. The fight/flight/freeze mechanism is there to protect us and keep us alive. It is rooted in survival. When something looks, smells, or sounds like danger, our body may become fueled to run, fight or shut down. When memories get stuck in our body/mind system, this danger alarm can go off extensively and get stuck in a pattern. It is helpful to keep in mind that our experience is not who we are. We are much more than our experience. There is more at the core of who we are.

Sometimes we lose our way, and lose track of who we are or what is at our core. Having a spiritual practice can assist us in developing humility and compassion, and expand our vision, allowing us to see a larger picture. This provides a framework that can help to bring us back to our compass of insight, and the calm, nurturing practice of compassion.

Why do we get triggered in relationships? Because there is vulnerability in relationship, and the closer, and more intimate and invested the relationship is, the more we can get triggered. Crazy, isn't it? This is when the dance may falter in its grace. Yet, when we do get triggered, this can be a tremendous opportunity for learning and healing. If we take that opportunity and allow ourselves to be vulnerable and have the courage to ride through it with humility, we can learn more about ourselves and others, and deepen our trust and our bond. Within our closest bonds, trauma and pain will surface because we are vulnerable. Holding compassion for our own heart and for the heart of our loved one is instrumental in deepening our level of trust and safety. When we relax into this with trust and compassion, and hold the insight of our own heart and truth, we can help each other grow with love. This way we can encourage each other to be more secure in being ourselves and working together collaboratively. When we open ourselves up with compassion, we can begin to move forward. As we practice loving compassion in our love relationship, it is possible to support each other in healing. There is the possibility of building greater resilience and hope. With the dance of an interweaving between compassion and insight, and loving communication, it is possible to create dance moves that help us grow and strengthen our character, enjoying the chemistry in the interaction. This kind of dance is a powerful, protective process that can increase our level of safety, sustainability, learning and contentment in our partnership.

Both the practice of compassion and insight requires conscious, loving awareness and communication. This loving awareness begins with the self-awareness of what we tell ourselves in our own mind, and how we communicate with others. Applying the compass of our insight can guide us in setting healthy boundaries, making clear decisions, and in creating a safety net in which we can explore, play and be safe to be loving. In the beginning of first contact with someone, we are sensing and assessing who this person is, and how we resonate with them. Our response may range from attraction to repulsion. Early on, if we pay attention to our inner signals, we can determine what kind of chemistry there is. Is there attraction, or repulsion? Or is it a combination? Is the chemistry sustainable, or fleeting, or toxic? We may have a mix of attraction and gut feelings that give off some alarms that we need to explore. We may doubt ourselves, pushing these signals under the rug. In my own experience, and from many stories of people I have worked with, there can be the experience of someone who appears to be a very nice person, who suddenly flips behavior and becomes disrespectful or abusive. This is deeper than chemistry; this is related to character. Looking back, we can often find red or yellow flags that we may have swept away from our awareness. As these flags come up, we may question if these alarms are more about me or them or both? Listening to our gut and using our insight guides us in establishing safety so that we are able to relax and enjoy ourselves and each other. It is like the awareness of a dancer who is grounded in their body, and able to navigate the space around them comfortably, with grace. Insight can guide our choices to align with what works for us and what does not work for us. Insight arises from listening to our gut feelings and responding to them, wedding objectivity and compassion. Using insight as our compass can leads us in establishing our boundaries and communicating about boundaries in a respectful way. Practicing both insight and compassion sets the stage for building a genuine foundation of safety and trust.

Another area of insight is being aware of our own needs and challenges, and noticing but not being overtaken by our pain. Holding both compassion and insight, and taking steps to take care of ourselves, will assist us in feeling balanced and cared for. If we are not taking good care of ourselves, it is harder to receive love and care from others. It is more challenging for us to be at our best, and to feel strong and focused in our dance. Our ability to be present with others can be compromised. When we are compassionate and caring with our own way of caring for ourselves, we are in a more natural place to both give and receive love.

Healthy boundaries include holding compassion for ourselves and with others in our close relationships. When we use our insight for setting boundaries, we can establish them in a way that fits who we are. Practice taking care of yourself first, and then decide who you want to spend time with. Listen to your gut, and honor your feelings. Having a spiritual practice that resonates with us can assist us in being in a quiet, peaceful state within our heart and mind. Give yourself the permission to be more kind and loving in your internal dialogue with yourself. Love yourself and protect yourself with gentleness, patience and honesty.

Compassion is absolutely vital in a loving relationship. In a loving, committed partnership, the more compassion we can hold for each other, the smoother our dance can become. Practicing compassion makes room to deepen our connection and makes room for more playfulness. Compassion can lead us to settling into being more present with one another. Compassion is feeling for and with the other person.

How do we practice this? One way is to remember that we all suffer. The awareness of suffering helps us to know that even if our perception tells us something like 'they have an easy life' or, 'they have it all together' we can know that we each have our own story. Our own challenge is to deal with the pain in our lives. We are not alone in that. This doesn't mean we need to act out our pain, and hurt ourselves or others. Instead, we can take a breath, and consciously practice compassion. If we believe we are the only ones who suffer, or that we suffer more than others, it can be a challenge to get out of ourselves and feel for someone else. With compassion we can feel for and appreciate different experiences.

A useful idea to keep in mind is that we each have unique gifts. In other words, we have our own way of seeing, thinking, feeling, expressing, and we have something unique to contribute. This helps us to stay curious and not fall into assumption, or thinking something like, 'it would be easier if they were more like me' or 'they are doing it wrong' or some other assumption or projection that gets in the way of compassion. This comes into play in all relationships, from parent to child, to love partners, to friends and work partners. When we hold the balance between knowing each of us has something unique to offer, and we each have our own unique challenges, we are in a good position to be able to collaborate. This brings us to the paradigm of 'power over, versus power with'. Acting out of fear and control, the tendency is to attempt to take power over others, and our communication can become rigid, manipulative or judgmental. If we are unconscious dancers, and mostly reacting, rather than being conscious and loving dancers, or if we give our power away, neither holding our ground in our bodies or opening to sharing with others, we will not be finding much joy or flow in our dance. We may lose our footing and fall or bump into a wall or another person and get bruised. As we become more aware of ourselves and others, we can hold our ground, recognize other dancers, and notice how we both move and interact.

When we take a stance of sharing and give and take, and take care of each other, we are able to operate with collaboration. This is a mutually beneficial dance. Approaching love like a dance can serve to get us flowing and moving and being centered in our bodies, more fully interacting with the space around us. Now we can be playful and enjoy our dance with a partner!

Start where you are. This is part of compassion, allowing ourselves to begin, exactly where we are and being present for ourselves. Reflect on what boundaries you need in your life right now, and see how you can honor that. Take a minute to feel compassion for yourself, in all aspects. Picture yourself at ease, comfortable in your body, centered and grounded. Imagine developing more conscious communication in the 'Dance of Love'. Consciously see yourself. Give yourself compassion, and then extend this to the people you love. Imagine creating a sacred space in which you are free to be yourself. See yourself in a loving space and state of mind and heart, fully grounded in your body. See yourself as free to dance with spirit and joy from the inside out, as your energy and the playfulness of movement becomes more expressed.

We can apply the practice of compassion and insight in developing a framework for safety and containment. With these elements of healthy relationship, we are in a better position to unravel stuck patterns and to navigate more sustainable communication and collaboration. This paves the way for a more conscious, intentional way of creating and building healthy relationship, and this strengthens both our individual resilience and relationship resilience.

What does it mean to come from our heart in a wise, calm way? It is not the place of emotion, survival, or triggers. It is that quiet, home in our heart, the place where we can relax and know that we can start with our breath and our heartbeat, a place we can always come home to. This is why we practice meditation and prayer. This is why we play music, make art or walk in nature. This is why we dance and make love. These can all be ways to come home to the center of our heart.

Here is a simple way to consciously center into your own heart. With your arms straight down, and your hands facing out, bring your arms up over your head until your hands come together. Now, bring your hands down in a prayer position, in front of your heart, at the center of your chest and say, "I am at home in my heart. I am here, centered in my body. I am at home in my heart." Breathe in the awareness that you can accept yourself with peace and compassion. Breathe out the awareness that you can have compassion for the Earth, and all beings. Know that you are part of nature and that you are here, at home in the center of your heart. Breathe in the hope and inspiration from the heavens, from the cosmos, from higher guidance. Center your attention and breathe through the calm, knowing, compassionate heart of being present.

The analytical mind can fall into self-criticism and judgement of others. There is the need to survive, to accomplish and move forward. This gives us the motivation to work, however; if we spend all our energy on this, and we forget to just be, then we lose our ability to be relaxed and joyful, to freely laugh, play and create. This is where child-like playfulness can bring us back to a state of being, in the flow of the dance of life.

As partners in love, we need to be able to relax and enjoy each other. We need to be able to communicate effectively and feel safe together. As loving partners, we can help each other to learn and grow, and enjoy life together. When there is misunderstanding or conflict, it can be challenging to find our way through such a labyrinth. Loving relationships can, like the story of Beauty and the Beast, allow us to transform our primal, beastly nature into a more refined and loving form of being, in which we can create more collaboration and deepen the enjoyment of the dance together. We can teach one another new dance moves. We can collaborate and create new steps so that we move more smoothly together.

One helpful form of communication between partners is to take turns making requests regarding communication. For example, ask for more encouraging feedback or time to talk over plans. Another suggestion is to plan entertaining things together. Being open to learning from each other keeps us humble and able to give and take in our growth, collaboratively. Honest, open communication and being vulnerable and sincere, provides an opportunity for conscious, constructive communication.

Every couple is unique and can create their own dance style of communication and shared action together.

In this dance of love, I invite you to practice more compassion for yourself and the people you love. The more attuned we are with our own core essence and with our heart of compassion, the more we can be present and resonate with our partner.

I invite you to consciously practice compassion in all of your relationships. I encourage you to use your inner compass of intuition and insight, and to enjoy the dance of communication, gradually incorporating more compassion and insight. This can deepen intimacy, build resilience, and contentment within the dynamic 'Dance of Love', in a conscious loving practice.

You can access bonuses, on the Dance of Love, where you can find an Invitation to the Dance, and The Dance of Love:The Dance of Life, at: http://blisslifepress.com/conscious-love/bonuses/

A Story of True Love…

Joni Young

"Own your Leadership,
Own your Happiness,
Own your Freedom,
and Own your Purposeful Prosperity.
Live each day with your most profound
intention, faith, and generosity.
Give credit where credit is due…May God be the Glory."
Joni Young

"Love is patient, love is kind. It does not envy, it does not boast, it is not proud. It does not dishonor others, it is not self-seeking, it is not easily angered, it keeps no record of wrongs. Love does not delight in evil but rejoices with the truth. It always protects, always trusts, always hopes, always perseveres. Love never fails."
1Cor 13:4-8

The garage door slammed shut. My heart sank and my blood froze. My husband had just left me. My heart ached so severely that I literally thought I was dying. At that very second, before I could react and run after the slammed door, my phone rang. For some reason, instead, I ran into the kitchen for the phone. At the other end of the phone, it was my friend, Khelin Young, later revealed to be my soul mate of this lifetime. Khelin and I had not spoken for many months and somehow that day and that very instant, he called me just to say "hi".

We had a very cordial friendship up to that point. Soon as I answered the phone and he asked, "How are you doing?" I broke down and said "my husband just left me."

The next few weeks' memories of the rest of that conversation and weeks thereafter were vague. I only recall the significant moment of that call. During those weeks, I relied on Diet Coke as my food source, most of the time. I lost over 20 lbs. and had a severe ulcer.

My daughter was six and my son was four months old. I had shut down my business while six weeks pregnant with my son. It was either keeping the baby safe or continuing my crazy work schedule. I chose the obvious and dropped everything to nurture my womb. So I had all the time in the world to fall into a deep depression when the tragedy hit.

Often times, my kids went to their grandparents because of my zombie state. The mansion I lived in was so lonely and cold. I could hear my own footsteps echo and it was like a field trip just to walk from my master bedroom to the garage. The silence drove me nearly crazy. I suffered from insomnia and could be up for weeks without a shut eye.

Before, when I had my thriving business, it seemed I had all the friends in the world. There was always an entourage around no matter where I went. Now, the realization came during the hardest time I'd ever experienced; those people were only around because I paid all the bills. I felt even lonelier, so the joke was on me. As the numbness grew more intensely, I became robotically productive. Within a seven-day span, I sold my mansion, and moved my kids and myself into our new small house. My mind swam as I anticipated of raising my kids alone and growing old by myself until I died. After all the assets settled and with divorce filed, I took off to Taiwan to clear my head and heart.

It didn't matter where I was, I couldn't escape the pain of my broken heart.

A few months went by. I finally got so sick of the silence, and called Khelin, who was known as a high performing party promoter in the LA area at that time. I figured anywhere was better than being at home in the evenings battling the dreaded silence and this hopeless hole in my heart. I basically invited myself to most of his functions and events. He was kind, never rejected me and always allowed me to tag along. One incident was especially memorable...

Love is kind...
One evening I called him as usual and said, "Wherever you are going tonight, I'm coming with you."

It was different that night because we went out to dinner at a nice restaurant, with a very nice and pretty young girl. I participated in the conversations and socialized unaware of what was really happening. The three of us went to a club after and I continued being clueless to what was really going on to focus on being unaware. Years later, I realized that Khelin was on a date with that girl and he was too nice to say "no" to me.

Love is patient...
Khelin stood by me as my beloved friend. He poured his unconditional kindness and compassion out to me, in a way I had never experienced. I was touched and healed by how he just cared for me with the utmost respect and honor. We shared many great conversations, deep thought exchanges, and enjoyed each other's friendship.

Love Protects...
I never developed an interest in cooking and went out of my way to avoid it. Often times when Khelin asked me what I ate, my answers were usually

Diet Coke or lemon cake, the two easiest items to purchase from the drive-through of a gas station. One day, Khelin came to my house with two bags of groceries and cooked a nice meal. I was so appreciative of the fresh warm food that I devoured everything.

That initiated the new tradition of him cooking for me at my house. Many years after we'd gotten married, I discovered he'd never cooked prior to that first incident of cooking for me. He took on an interest to learn and cook all kinds of exotic delicious meals inspired by my lack of cooking abilities. He couldn't stand the fact that I had made Diet Coke and lemon cake as my primary staples. He always said I was the one who inspired him to become such an amazing chef. Although flattered by this thought, I feel so blessed that his talents in flavoring were unfolded and my children and I have been the lucky taste testers through this yummy journey.

Love is Trust...
Many months went by, we became best friends and we talked about anything and everything. My best perk was him coming over to cook and learning from his wisdom. He had an incredible divine aura that could always hypnotically calm me.

One casual evening, we decided spontaneously to go to Shoreline Village in Long Beach. As we strolled along the Village, we came across a big sign that said, "Murder Mystery Dinner Cruise." We hopped on the cruise and had a fantastic time. I vividly remembered somehow my perception of him was different that night on the cruise. He seemed "kind of cute" to me. It was the strangest feeling because we were such great friends and I was so familiar with his presence. Unbeknownst to me, he felt butterflies in his stomach at that very same moment and was in utter shock when he realized he had fallen in love with me. In summary, we got hit by Cupid's arrows at the same time.

Love Perseveres...
Everything changed that night. We no longer could see each other from just the friendship perspective.

Khelin was orphaned at four years old. His family was among the elite of the elite in his home country of Cambodia. During the Vietnam War, his father who was a high-ranking General, was taken away and never came home. It was known that his father was executed. His mother was a doctor. When the war broke out, she opened her clinic to treat all the wounded and sick and depleted all of her medication supplies.

When she got sick with pneumonia, she died from lack of Penicillin. Khelin escaped with his uncle during the night on foot across the border to Thailand where they eventually immigrated to the U.S.

Life was rough and lonely as an orphan child. While living through the trauma of the war, losing his parents, and through many years afterward of endless nights of nightmares, Khelin had one great mission in life. It was to find his one true love, have his own family, and live happily ever after.

Khelin made it a priority to educate himself about love and relationships. He explored, experimented, and searched. Combined with his profound gift of wisdom from God at a young age and his tragic upbringing, his understanding and comprehension of human relationships grew by leaps and bounds. As a result, he continuously got disappointed with conversations, relationships, and felt a lack of belonging in this world.

In college, Khelin found God, got baptized, and immersed himself into the ministry life. While he was leading and mentoring a large group of students in the campus ministry, they often held discussions about dating and finding a wife. Khelin spoke out during one conversation to say he was frustrated with not being able to identify a suitable candidate to date for potential marital relationship. He declared that he would go outside the ministry and find his future wife in the marketplace, baptize her, then marry her.

Five years later, Khelin baptized me, proposed to me, and we got married three weeks thereafter.

Love never fails...
It was a lazy and casual afternoon; I was sitting on my couch relaxing. Khelin came up to me, got down on his knee, and opened up a little ring case. It was the perfect romantic setting. However, when I saw the ring, I fell to the floor. Shocked by the loud thump from my fall, his eyes opened really big and he fearfully asked me if I didn't like the ring. It was a beautifully designed butterfly ring made with marquise diamonds. After I fumbled around and picked myself up off the floor, I shared with him a flashback thought. When I was a little girl around nine years old in my home country Taiwan, one day I looked up at the sky and told God that someday I will marry the man who gives me a butterfly ring!.

I have always been fond of butterflies since I was a little girl. I used to chase after them and thought they are such beautiful creatures that represented natural beauty's transformations. They seemed so free and happy. This topic never came up during my interactions with Khelin over the years and he had no clue that I had such special connections with butterflies. He said that when he visited the jewelry store, among the many choices of rings, somehow the butterfly ring spoke out to him.

When I came to the reality that I had fallen in love with Khelin that first night after the Murder Mystery Cruise, I put my feelings for him inside a box and insisted on remaining friends. I refused to acknowledge the longing and love because I could not fathom another failure and heartbreak. The trauma was too deep and the wounds were too fresh. My plan after my divorce was to live out the rest of my life alone.

Although it was a stupid decision, it was a determination and vision I crafted for myself. I knew I had to be strong for my young children.

We went on for many months from best friends to intimacy. Due to my lack of dating experiences, I didn't even realize we were "dating." To me, he was home and I felt a sense of peace and safety when we were together. It all seemed so right. Our feelings grew stronger and stronger and I was happy. But I didn't understand it and didn't trust it.

One day, I discovered that I was pregnant. I was shocked and overjoyed at the same time. I felt a deep soul-tie with this baby as he brought me immense strength and happiness. I felt as though I received an injection of hope and purpose. When I shared this news with Khelin, I was prepared for his departure from my life. I thought it would scare him off. I had already convinced myself of this fact. However, when Khelin expressed how ecstatic he was and as he began to talk about our future together, I completely shut down. It was as though a tunnel caved in and I felt suffocated with fear.

I stopped all communications with him and pushed him away. Those days were absolutely horrifying because I drowned myself and Khelin in despair. Khelin called me day and night continuously pleading for a conversation. Finally, I agreed to meet him. I told myself that I must send him away now so I could protect myself from ever facing the pain of a broken heart. I was determined to raise this baby and my other children alone. I did not believe in love, although I was so much in love with him.

When we finally met up, all walls broke down and I melted into his gentle, kind, and loving spirit. We both cried and couldn't bear the thought of ever being apart. Love triumphed. I chose love, at that instant. I chose to follow my heart. He moved into my house and we began a family together.

One agreement, more like a one-sided agreement on my part, that we made was that we would never get married. I was adamant that I'd never marry again. To me, marriage was a bad word. It represented suffering, betrayal, and lack of love. This was a hurt in Khelin's heart which he never bestowed upon me. He just gently accepted it and loved me and my children unconditionally.

Khelin demonstrated his selflessness by diving deeply into his fatherly role. He loved my daughter and my son wholeheartedly and cared for them as though they were his own. Many nights he woke to take care of my young son as I slept through the nights. He played with my six-year-old daughter and connected with her every day. He was far better at being a father than I was at being a mother. He nurtured me and treated me like a queen throughout my pregnancy. I was happy. Yet I still didn't understand it, or more likely, I didn't trust it.

Love is new life...
The day my new son was born was one of the happiest moments of my life. I felt loved and content. We named him "Will" as we believe he came to us as God's will. Although I couldn't fathom God's love at this time, I got a glimpse of His mercy through Khelin's love and the gift of my son Will.

During the months following Will's birth, Khelin began to re-engage with the topic of marriage. He had never been married before and being a husband was one of his lifelong dreams. My heart was so fragile that I refused to even get close to this topic. I knew I was hurting him, but I didn't know how to fix it.

This was also the time that we began to attend church and a series of bible studies. Khelin was baptized in college and acquired a deep connection with God. He led a college campus ministry with over 50 students at one point. During a crisis and major leadership transition period, several mishandled incidences severely damaged Khelin's faith and caused him to leave the church. About five years later we started to study the bible and Khelin immediately felt the convictions of God's doctrines and rekindled his faith.

One day he came home, packed his bags and moved out. He said he must follow God's decrees and honor me. This was obviously a shock to me as I didn't understand why God would want me to be unhappy. All the feelings of abandonment and betrayals quickly crept up and overwhelmed me. I began to question God, His Word, and all the brothers and sisters from church who were so lovingly trying to support me through this. I became argumentative during bible studies and interpreted all scriptures to convince myself that God was against me.

Spiritually, Khelin and I were on a different path which I was completely clueless about. I was just absorbed in the sorrows of his decision to leave us. In all reality, he did not leave us. He continued to come home to spend time with the kids and cook for us. He continued to love us the same way, just from a purity standpoint with me. I didn't understand or comprehend the situation. I thought we were supposed to be a family.

Khelin secretly made a vow to God, that he'd dedicate his life to Him and be His faithful servant, and that if I did not accept God into my life, then he'd give up on our relationship and remain the father of our children from a distance. He cried to God to change my heart. He prayed for me and my salvation day after day.

One Sunday morning while debating whether I should attend church service or not, I randomly opened the bible. It was the first chapter of the Book of Job. Prior to this, the bible seemed like a foreign language book and I never coherently comprehended what it was really saying. Somehow that morning, as I dived into the scriptures, it came alive to me and I soaked in every word and understood everything. Tears burst out uncontrollably and I sobbed non-stop. I finished reading the entire Book of Job and was an utter mess. It was my very first encounter with the Holy Spirit and the presence of God. I felt His love for me and His acknowledgement of me.

I went to church and informed Khelin that I was ready to be baptized. Despite his jaw dropping expression, he calmly hugged me and arranged for my baptism that following Wednesday evening. He was alongside of me with the minister. Khelin prayed for me and then proceeded to submerge me in the water. There I was, a new born Christian.

Three weeks later, he proposed. When I saw the butterfly ring, I had no doubt in my mind that I was supposed to marry this man. We got married three weeks later with over 250 people's blessings at our wedding. It was one of the happiest days of my life.

This was true fate at its best; God's plan revealed in real time. It marked the declaration that Khelin made just five years' prior... that he'd find his future wife, baptize her, and marry her.

We were living our dreams. Khelin found his one true love and finally has a family of his own. I was happy.

When you find true love, all things are possible...

We started a business together ten months after we got married. It was an import/export wholesale lumber business. We poured in everything we had and built it from the ground up. I was the CEO of our company and Khelin was responsible for sales/marketing/design. In four years' time, we outgrew our own projections and became a well sustaining west coast regional supplier for the trade. 2008 rolled around and I noticed the housing market's downward spiral. Many of our competitors were either shrinking rapidly or had gone out of business. As I made the strategic decision to play offense and launched our biggest expansion campaign across the country, I was diagnosed with breast cancer.

I chose to continue with our expansion project while going through eleven surgeries including mastectomy, and chemotherapy. Despite others' suggestions to hold off on our business expansion, I knew that if we didn't move forward, our company would dwindle and not survive the economic crash. Having the responsibilities of our shareholders' and team members' wellbeing on my shoulders, I stuck it through and just focused on one day at a time.

Khelin supported every decision I made and worked around my hospital visits, surgery schedules, and chemotherapy sessions. I continued to work and remain active with our business. I never knew how tough it was for Khelin during those days. He never once complained or questioned my decisions for our company. He stood by me, supported me, and took care of me. He cried in secret and I never saw him shed a tear in front of me or our children. He was my pillar and my knight in shining armor.

I was bald, scarred, and physically unable to be his wife during those months. Through it all, my biggest take away memory from those eighteen months was that my husband made me feel like the most beautiful woman in the whole wide world. He loved me, honored me, and encouraged me deeply and graciously every day.

As for our business, it grew exponentially and we went national and international. We had distribution centers across the country, over 8,000 customers throughout the U.S., Canada, Cayman Islands, and Bermuda. Our annual revenues were in the $20-million range and we were known as one of the most reputable brand name supplier among our trade.

Years went by, and all the business travels, meetings, business demands, and family obligations consumed us. On the surface, we were successful, respected, and wealthy. Internally, our souls were dying and our relationship was being torn day by day. I was miserable and so was he. We had lost our way from each other. There seemed to be layers and layers of iron bricks between us. We loved each other but felt far from each other. He was close but I couldn't connect with him anymore. We fought frequently and the bulk of the time this was due to factors relevant to other people.

Finally, enough was enough. We began to fight back. After a few years of intentional conversations and struggles to rise above the problems, we made a decision. We identified the root cause of our barriers and we fought it head on. We got clear, real clear. We chose love, whatever it took; we chose each other.

We decided to sell our business and start over. It had become the cancer of our love. We set a goal to sell it within three months. It seemed like an impossible task at the moment due to the magnitude of our business. We vowed to God that we would dedicate our lives to serve His purpose and asked Him for blessings. We sold the business in four months and walked away. This was spring of 2014.

God blessed us because we chose to be faithful to each other; we chose love over money, power, and fame.

We took a year off to travel with our family, spent quality time with each other, and most importantly, I followed Khelin's lead to pursue our much-needed intimacy with the Holy Spirit. The closer we got to God, the closer Khelin and I got to each other. Before long, we fell in love again. That feeling of excitement and butterflies in the stomach came back again. I couldn't wait to see him every day. And his cooking became more and more amazing. I could taste his love in every dish. Khelin intricately crafted our new life with romance, tenderness, and amazing intimacy. I made it my priority to honor, respect, and trust him with all my heart.

During our year's rest, I received many proposals for business opportunities. People even chased me down while on a family vacation in Taiwan. I was amused and flattered at the same time. While it was my nature to jump into another business, I respected my husband's thoughts of putting all business ideas behind the back burners and just focus on our relationship with God, with each other, and with our children.

When time came for us to embark on our new business ventures, we independently chose to go after our passions and maximize on our God-given talents. Khelin launched a Relationship and Wealth Coaching business. He soon attracted a tribe of clients who adored him for who he really is and allowed him to help them at his best level. He has repaired marriages, salvaged broken relationships, and taught many people his success principles of "How to Fall in Love with Your Spouse Every Day." One of the main causes for marital issues is financial stress. So this has been an area of focus for Khelin in his teachings as well. In addition, God had also blessed Khelin with phenomenal opportunities to establish his own investment portfolio. It has given our family a new light and hope for financial independence.

As for me, I struggled initially with getting inspirations of building a new business. I've successfully built six, seven and eight-figure businesses over the last three decades of my entrepreneurial journey, so the idea of going to build another business just did not seem all that enticing to me. I had no doubt that whatever business I chose to build, it would be successful because this has been my expertise. However, my fear was to build a business without it reflecting my true calling.

An idea came to me as I explored my "why" and my gifts. I thought of helping other entrepreneurs build their businesses. Through casual conversations the word got out that Joni was out of retirement and now consulting with businesses. Some interests came and I followed through. Business building and strategic problem solving have been my specialties so results generated pretty quickly. I acquired some high performance corporate clients working with CEOs and Executive Teams on leadership trainings and business growth strategies. Within a few months, I launched a six-figure consulting firm. What a miraculous blessing!

One client increased their revenues by 87% in just 60 days of following my coaching and mentoring. Another client saved about $1-million dollars from my strategic operational re-structuring. And, one client increased their accounts receivable efficiencies by 750% which translated to a lot MORE money in their pockets. Wow! What a privilege to have the opportunity to serve others in this scope and watch them soar! This...is my true calling...being a CEO Coach.

As for philanthropy work, my dream has been to empower women around the globe to help transform their lives after domestic abuse or breast cancer, utilizing the vehicle of entrepreneurship. I was also given a divine vision of collaborating with global initiatives to free women from sex trade in Southeast Asia.

It is truly intriguing how the law of attraction works. Once I identified my purpose and calling, the paths and doorways began to come my way. I've connected with influential organizations and individuals relevant to these platforms. This included a recent encounter with some amazing women leaders worldwide. At this event, I also got to sit in on a United Nations Foundation's presentation about their global initiatives specifically for women entrepreneurs.

My husband and I raised a child from Kenya for the past eight years. We contributed and served under different charitable capacities during our international travels. Philanthropy work has been a conscious part of our lifestyle. It is a shared passion that makes our love stronger and helps us share that love into the world. We involved ourselves whenever and wherever we could.

Love, success, and philanthropy...You can have it all. The journey is very real and never ending. Be aware of your path. Get clear on what you want. Set an action plan. Seek out a coach/mentor to help you hone in on the specific targeted guidance in whatever area you may need. The best investment you can make is in yourself. Then dive in. Just go for it. One day, your life will flash before your eyes, so make sure it's worth watching. It's better to get wounded a million times and remain standing at the end than never to seek out the possibilities of your victories.

A word of caution; do not chase money. Get clear on your inner "burning desire." Set sail towards it. Then you will attract abundance. Money is only an energy source and it CANNOT buy love.

Blessings and Cheers to True Love.

Please go to http://blisslifepress.com/conscious-love/bonuses/ to download my bonus gift, "Secrets to Owning Your Love & Success"!

"For I know the plans I have for you," declares the Lord, "plans to prosper you and not to harm you, plans to give you hope and a future. Then you will call on me and come and pray to me, and I will listen to you. You will seek me and find me when you seek me with all of your heart. I will be found by you," declares the Lord, "and will bring you back from captivity."
Jeremiah 29:11-14 NIV

How to Open Your Heart to True Love

Dr. Sky Blossoms

"When your heart is open to love, you become ultimately attractive,
unapologetically authentic,
and your life turns into an ecstatic stream of synchronicities."
Sky Blossoms

You and millions of others on our planet want to love and be loved. Then why is it so challenging for most people to experience meaningful and fulfilling relationships that last? And, why do so many people feel lonely and desperate for affection? And, most importantly, how can you solve the love puzzle in your life, so that you can have real soulful connection, passion, and a relationship that makes you come alive?

It's easy to blame loneliness and emptiness inside on not having the right mate. However, everyone knows the timeless wisdom that what you put out, you get back. Virtually every philosophy has said the same thing, but in different words. You are the cause, and the circumstances of your life are the effect. Every situational challenge in our lives, whether it's a relationship, health, or a financial issue, is a mere consequence of our state of being. You don't have to depend on anyone to improve your life. Therefore, in this chapter, we will not look anywhere outside of yourself for solutions. I'll show you how to tap into your own hidden potential to achieve the results that you desire.

Do you know the feeling of being in love? If you have experienced it even once, you would remember how your happiness was overflowing, and you wanted to share it with everyone. Your heart was ready to jump out of your chest, and you wanted to hug the whole world. You were forgiving, optimistic, and elated. Circumstances were lining up miraculously, and your life felt magical, because love puts you in concert with the force of life.

What if you could feel like that every day, regardless of whether you have a mate or not? In this chapter, you will learn the secrets to unlocking the infinite supply of love within the treasury of your own heart, and how to unleash your natural charm, so that you can become magnetic and irresistible. Your own light, shining brightly, will enable you to stand out from the crowd effortlessly, and you will become visible to your ideal mate.

Throughout our journey together, we will employ research, science, and spiritual wisdoms to propel you forward. You are not the first one to walk the path, and those who came before you left clues. I have been in your shoes, and went from loneliness, and even depression, divorces and heartbreaks, to living a life full of miracles, love, and joy. Prepare to have fun, and to unleash the best version of yourself yet!

Discovery
My bare feet caressed the dry, dusty soil of the Arizona desert, while my mind was racing for a solution. Here I was, in a beautiful Eden, where I was supposed to enjoy healing hot springs and have a great time. Instead, I felt pressured and frustrated.

The smallest things in relationships can knock you off balance. This time the quandary was super simple, yet unpleasant. I was hungry and wanted to grab a bite and return to soak. My friend Inna proposed a group gathering for dinner, and insisted that we wait for everyone. Her request meant going against my desire to be in a pool, and meant to and then cleaning, instead. As Inna kept insisting on the idea of the group dinner, I felt resentful towards the expectation that I should comply, and I was afraid of being judged as selfish if I didn't.

As I was walking towards the kitchen, I asked myself the question that I find to be the most productive when faced with a choice. "What do I really want?" The answer that emerged was life-changing...

I realized that all I wanted was to love. I did not want my friend to behave differently, nor did I want any changes in the circumstance. I just wanted to love everyone wholeheartedly, completely, and openly, regardless of the situation. I didn't want anyone's behavior, looks, or decisions to impede my ability to open my heart and to embrace them completely. I wanted to honor their freedom to decide for themselves, and to honor my freedom to choose for me.

I wanted to release my own judgments of myself and others, because it became clear that the source of my discomfort had nothing to do with my friend's demand. I used her behavior as the reason to close my heart and to allow fear. While I was uncomfortable with her judging me, I judged her for being pushy...

Can I love her just as much, regardless of her expectations of me and her approval or disapproval of my actions? Can I love and embrace others even if they don't love me? Can I completely adore a person whom my mind perceives as unattractive? Can I stay loving when someone is rude to me? Can I observe violence, and still love the "offender," despite their inhumane actions?

My heart was screaming a passionate "YES!" but I had no idea how to accomplish this degree of unconditional love. This new desire to love opened the door to real freedom for me. Over the next few years, the answers were coming in increments, like pieces of a puzzle. And today I can see through the illusionary veil of my mind into the truth of my heart and consciously open to love no matter what.

True Love
Even though to love and to be loved is a fundamental human desire, most people get confused about love. Infatuation, lust, or empathy are often mistaken for love. Many people even believe that love can cause heartbreaks.

Love cannot be painful. When you love, it is a blissful experience. Pain comes when you try to stop loving, thereby denying your very nature. Unfulfilled expectations are the source disappointments and sorrows. When you close your heart, that's when it hurts.

It's common to believe that unconditional love is inaccessible to humans, and that only God or spiritual masters are capable of it. While it's true that most people don't know how to stay open to unconditional love, everyone has experienced it, even if for a brief moment. Moreover, anything that is conditional is not really love, and ought to have a different name.

Conscious Love Relationship is the playground of unconditional love. It's not for the timid. Peeling the layers of resistance and opening ever so fully, takes courage and dedication. Love is not something you get in a relationship, it is something you discover within your own heart and learn to share. When your lover shares her heart with you, you receive her love not because you need it, but because by graciously receiving, you are offering your mate a delightful opportunity to give.

Love does not imply relationships. And, while love is unconditional, relationships are conditional.

Since love comes from within, you can increase your heart opening and love everyone, without exceptions. I demonstrate this in my live workshops, where I help my students fall in love with a complete stranger in less than 30 minutes. However, a sustainable union requires more than love. Compatibility is essential. The feeling of affinity, physical chemistry, similar interests, values, and lifestyle choices, are examples of compatibility. Yet, neither one of them should be mistaken for love.

If two people love each other, but are not compatible, their relationship turns into an emotional roller coaster, with a lot of drama. If there is compatibility, but no love and passion, a couple becomes best friends who are living together, which makes their union comfortable, but dull and unfulfilling. In order to live and co-create in harmony, you need to have both love and compatibility.

Choose every relationship in your life wisely. Also know that you are being chosen. In your love life, you and your mate get to choose one another, every moment of every day. And, it is your responsibility to show up at your best, so that it's easy for your lover to choose you over and over again.

I titled my first #1 bestselling book "Best Thing Ever," because I discovered that happy couples often say to each other "You're the best thing that ever happened to me." Imagine having a mate who never ceases to amaze you, a person who is constantly growing, learning, and becoming more... And, you are getting an "upgraded" version of them every day. Wouldn't it be awesome to fall in love with your partner more and more as years go by, simply because they become more lovable every day?

What if you were the mate who keeps getting better? Your ultimate contribution is being the best ever version of you. Get clear on what that looks like, and do everything you can to embody your greatness.

Remember, neither you nor your mate is obligated to be with each other forever, even if you are in a committed relationship. In order to stay happily together, your union needs to be nurtured, and you need to keep growing and stepping up. Consider being with your beloved a privilege, and don't take it for granted, even for a second. People in your intimate circle deserve the best of you, especially your partner.

Co-creating a love relationship based on pure unconditional love, fueled by passion, and spiced up by playfulness and seduction, grants you an experience of Heaven on Earth. Imagine waking up every morning feeling cherished and completely adored by your partner. What would it feel like to be laughing together until your cheeks are hurting? What if you were turned on by your mate like never before, where even the slightest touch or look would get you aroused? Wouldn't it be great to be proud of your lover, and to feel lucky to have him in your life?

The great news is that you can have a relationship that is extraordinary in every way! During my research, I found and interviewed dozens of couples who enjoy Conscious Love Relationships. They have one thing in common. Each partner devoted time and effort to cultivating self-acceptance, releasing holdbacks, and opening to love. The moment each individual felt happy with their own life and released the urge to look for an outer source of fulfillment, they met each other.

Opening Your Heart
Your capacity to feel and experience love is proportionate to the opening of your heart. What people call "falling in love," is simply a spontaneous heart opening, which helps you feel the deliciousness of your own love flowing. Since most people don't understand the process, they give the credit for this delightful feeling to others (lover, child, pet, etc.), which may create dependency, or even obsession.

If you come across someone whose heart is already open, like a puppy or a baby, or a happy person, you don't feel the need to protect yourself from them. Your natural inclination to open to love takes over, allowing for a blissful experience of affection. That's why innocence is so attractive, because it's not threatening, and it serves as an invitation to connect. Consequently, if your heart is open, you become very lovable and inspire others to open as well.

The reverse is true also. When one person is defensive and closed off, it becomes very challenging for another to remain open and to embrace them. Most people use the behavior of others as a valid reason to close off. This is how pain gets perpetuated, and how a heart gets closed off in the first place. "He betrayed me! How can I love him?" "She is so selfish! Why should I like her?" Your mind's judgments are there to protect you from potential pain. Yet, they block the flow of love which is the real source of pain.

Imagine being a young, innocent child and you get yelled at, or criticized, or someone is mean to you. It's shocking at first, and you do not understand how they could do this to you. Since there is no explanation or guidance on how to process your pain, you cope with your sorrow. Then another painful situation occurs, and you start developing defensive walls to avoid more hurt. You adapt your behavior: play small, hold back, and express yourself selectively, or to the contrary, openly rebel and thereby get yourself in trouble.

After years of coping with pain, a person may disconnect from their true desires and may lose their sense of authenticity, and even their sense of identity. A mere shadow of themselves, they feel increasingly lonely and empty inside. They try to fill the void with food, or drugs, distract themselves from this pain by gambling or watching too much TV, or resort to prescription medications to feel a little better.

People with closed hearts experience low self-esteem, which prompts repellent behaviors like neediness, hesitation, dependency, jealousy, need for validation, and possessiveness. Since all of these are unattractive, they turn people off, and the cycle of loneliness and pain continues.

If insecurities are bleeding, it indicates an unhealed emotional wound. That is why transcending old sorrows and releasing emotional baggage is essential to cultivating self-love and enabling happiness. When a heavy burden of the past has been removed, your heart will naturally open to love. And you will recapture child-like innocence and charm.

Releasing Emotional Baggage
If you are like most people, you clean your body and your house much more often than you clear your emotions. Have you noticed how expressive young children are? They yell, simply because they feel like it.

If they are happy, they laugh out loud and jump up and down, if they are upset, they cry. As an adult, you are conditioned to suppress your emotions which keeps them stored in your system.

Unresolved traumas, shame, guilt, regrets, and perceived failures may accumulate in your psyche and body, resulting in dis-eases, stress and lack of mental focus. They cause emotional volatility and decrease performance. Your health and vitality, financial wellbeing, spirituality, and relationships are adversely affected by this burden. This load needs to be released in order for you to accept yourself completely and to love yourself unconditionally.

In relationships, any past traumas, insecurities, or hidden fears will inevitably trigger defenses. Subconscious self-preservation will cause you to contract and close your heart. When your heart is closed, authentic and sincere connection to a partner becomes impossible. That's when people get into frustrating arguments and get stuck in a loop of disagreements and misunderstanding.

Letting go of emotional baggage was the common denominator among all of the conscious couples that I have interviewed. Each partner, independently from the other, had gone on a spiritual journey of healing from past pains and limiting beliefs.

Releasing emotional baggage is an essential step to succeeding in EVERY area of your life. Limiting beliefs are defense mechanisms. They hold a promise of protecting you from experiencing pain in the future. That's why your mind eagerly adopts them, and this is also the reason why they may be challenging to release. For example, "I'm not smart enough." This belief will keep a person from expressing their opinion thereby eliminating a potential disapproval of others. It is important to transcend the pain, before a limiting belief can be reframed. Metaphorically speaking, you need to remove the shark, before you ask a person to swim in open water.

Imagine letting go of all shame, guilt, regrets, grudges, rejection, and heartbreaks that you've experienced. You would emerge feeling lighter and stronger than ever. You would have a new sense of freedom and empowerment. And you would understand yourself better. This release would give you ease and clarity.

I guide my clients through a personalized clearing process, where they let go of emotional blocks and re-capture confidence, restore vitality, and discover more self-love. This is a profoundly transformational experience, which results in:
· Natural confidence
· Better relationships
· More energy
· Mental clarity
· Laser focus
· Increased earning potential
...and much more

You can find many tools to help dissolve your triggers and release your baggage. These are just a few of the tools that I employ in my practice: Intuitive Healing, Strategic Intervention, NLP (Neurolinguistic Programming), EFT (Emotional Freedom Technique), Reiki, Behavioral Psychology, Neuroscience, etc. Whether you prefer traditional counseling and therapy, or alternative holistic approaches like hypnosis or plant medicine, I invite you to use the methods you resonate with, and to heal your emotional wounds as soon as possible.

To give you a head start, in the bonus section you will get my FREE downloadable toolkit to release emotional baggage. It includes step-by-step guidance on how to uncover your holdbacks and permanently release them. Go to: http://blisslifepress.com/conscious-love/bonuses/

Most people don't like it when their buttons get pushed. I invite you to welcome the experience, because it makes you aware of the button. It is your responsibility to dissolve the button, rather than trying to demand that no one touches it. The truth is, as long as you have buttons, there will be people who'll push them.

This is an ongoing process. I'm not suggesting that one day you'll wake up invincible, and that no one can ruffle your feathers. At the same time, taking ownership of your reactions grants you freedom. When you realize that it's not other people's behavior that's painful, but the way you perceive it, you can change your response.

It is important to note that when an emotional trauma is fully healed, all the symptoms cease. You do not get triggered anymore. For example, a person who experienced infidelity, after resolving the emotional trauma associated with the incident, will be able to trust a new partner completely, and have a loyal relationship.

Give yourself the gift of freedom, and not only you will be happier, more attractive and confident, but you will also be more loving towards others. If you are a giver by nature, then it's your duty to heal your pains, so that they don't hinder your contribution to others.

Especially if you have children or planning to have them, releasing your emotional baggage is vital to being a good role model. Didn't your parents pass on to you some of their sorrows? The nature of limiting beliefs is self-perpetuating, and those who carry them inevitably try to pass them onto others. Clear your limitations to avoid contaminating the minds of those you love.

When you release your emotional baggage, you no longer harbor blame or victimhood. You become more peaceful and responsive versus reactive. You will feel comfortable in your own skin and become naturally magnetic.

Maintaining Heart Opening
When my desire to love unconditionally became clear, I had no idea on how to keep my heart open, regardless of the circumstances. The first insight I received and put to practice was, 'Respect Other People's Choices'. This does not mean liking or approving their actions. It's simply an acknowledgement that everyone is free to choose for themselves, and they are responsible for their decisions.

The question that audiences often ask when I speak live is, "What if some choices are harmful to others?" It is very possible. Even seemingly innocent actions, like using toilet paper, may be harmful to trees, which may have been cut to make the product. Everything has cause and effect. At the same time, only you are in control of your choices. Any attempts to control the behaviors of others will result in frustration and feeling powerless, because it never works. Moreover, it infringes on their freedom.

The second insight was, 'Practice Compassion'. People offer harmful or hostile behavior when they are in pain. This does not justify destructive actions. At the same time, simply trust that every person wants to feel better, and they do the best they can. You may not fully understand another person's motives, or relate to, or grasp their perspective, nor do you need to. Choose to love them anyway. Not because their behavior deserves love, but because that's who you are. If you dislike, resent, or fear them, you contribute to the cycle of pain. If you open your heart and love them, you soothe their pain and help to stop the suffering for all. Perpetuate love, not hurt.

Love me when I least deserve it,
because that's when I really need it.
—Swedish Proverb

The third insight is, 'Cultivate Appreciation'. The vibration of appreciation is one of the purest vibrations available to us, and it's akin to the vibration of unconditional love. When being loving is challenging, do your best to be appreciative.

Master Your Communication and Seduction Skills
In order to connect with others heart-to-heart and maintain your own

heart opening, it's important to be a good communicator. Communication is likely the most valuable skill in life. This is the link between you and others. Your self-perception is the result of your communication with yourself. The quality of your communication determines the quality of your relationships. Dedicating your time and effort into improvement of your communication skills is a worthwhile investment, which pays dividends for a lifetime.

As you may know, verbal exchange is only a small part of communication. Literally everything about you sends messages: your demeanor, outfit, fragrance, body language, facial expressions, hair style etc.

I encourage you to increase your awareness of the communication signals you send and to become more attuned to the signals you are receiving. Pay close attention to people and observe their responses. You'll be able to pick up on hidden subtleties of their tone of voice and mannerisms, and learn to read between the lines. You'll know if someone's telling the truth, or if a person is uncomfortable. You can determine if your conversational partner is actively engaged with you or distracted, if they are interested or bored, if they are irritated or pleased.

Your active listening, full presence, and keen attention will give you an upper hand in every interaction and provide you with a unique insight into the person with whom you are conversing. Never again, will you ask your mate a silly question, "Honey, are you okay?" because you will know the answer, and you will be able to offer a more personable approach. Your communication will be deeper and more meaningful. After decades of studying various aspects of communication, I can offer you one piece of advice; stay away from pigeon-holing systems, like personality types. While your mind will be busy classifying someone, you'll miss the opportunity to connect with that person's heart.

Think about it. There are millions of different trees on our planet. The logical mind wants to organize the information and break all trees into types or categories, compartmentalizing nature in order to make sense of it. Your heart, on the other hand, wants to connect with each tree and to love it regardless of its type.

Don't reduce a person down to an astrology sign, or a personality type. See and embrace the entirety of them. Follow your heart in connecting with people. Look into their eyes and attempt to see their soul. Your intuition is the most valuable communication tool. Learn to listen to it and trust it.

The Secret Weapon...
Would you like to know the secret weapon for crazy passion, fun, excitement, and romance in your relationship? This is so much fun; I couldn't resist sharing it with you! Drum roll please...
You are about to discover the most misunderstood, yet powerful tool for

keeping your chemistry on fire— Seduction.

Seduction is your ability to create an emotional experience in another person and evoke a desire.

It is invaluable, not only in the early days of your love affair, but in the long run as well. In the past, you may have experienced strong attraction which diminished over time. Chemistry requires polarity. Just as the magnets get pulled together due to the opposite charges, the masculine and feminine ends of the spectrum need to be pronounced in order for magnetism to occur naturally. Since both men and women have masculine and feminine energies within them, getting conscious control of these forces affords you sustainable and juicy connection, and makes your intimate dance fun, pleasurable, and effortless.

Seduction means being deliciously attractive in who you are and what you are all about. It is NOT manipulation, but an artful orchestration of your interaction. And foreplay begins way prior to your first kiss. It starts before you say "hello."

Below are three proven tips which you can put to practice right away.

Tip #1: Create an Emotional Experience
Upon meeting, most people keep their communication at a surface level— small talk and Q&A ping-pong, which is a mere exchange of information. This may help you to learn a person's history or interests, but there is little, if any, emotional impact. Your ability to create an emotional experience is the key to attraction and seduction.

Consider this: What would you rather do, attend a very informative lecture or see an exciting movie which makes you laugh, cry, and get thrilled? Would you rather eat a bar that contains all of the vitamins and nutrition for your body, or enjoy an artfully prepared meal that smells, looks, and tastes like heaven? The more senses are tickled, the more vibrant and memorable your experience will be.

I invite you to have conversations that matter to you. Talk about things you are passionate about, ask questions that you really want to know the answers to, and express yourself freely. Don't be afraid to stir disagreements, for they afford you and your mate an opportunity to see a new perspective. Don't try to keep things smooth, rather keep them interesting, fun, and exciting.

Pleasure is not always nice and sweet otherwise people wouldn't enjoy exploding things in computer games, or going to a shooting ranch, or car racing. There is a dark side to pleasure, which needs to be embraced and explored. If you pretend that it does not exist, feel ashamed of it, or suppress it in some way, it will rear its head as aggression or violence. Just as there is a range of flavors from sweet to spicy, and from bitter to sour, there is a range of human emotions. Flavors are experienced best in combination, and when the right balance and proportions are achieved. The same is true for emotional experiences. You want to mix them up for ultimate satisfaction.

Spice up your interactions with humor and spontaneity. Employ sensual attributes like food, touch, or fragrances. Make your communication intentional on every level and inspire laughter, surprise, adventure, or romantic cozy relaxation. The quality of the experience you create will determine a person's desire to spend more time with you. This holds true for every circumstance. Whether you are communicating with your lover, child, co-worker, or a perfect stranger, the way you make them feel is what they will remember. And if the feeling is stimulating or pleasurable, they will want more of it.

Enchantress
Her playful touch awakens your desire
Her voice and smile intoxicate your mind
Her ease and charm are things that you admire
Her depth and thoughtfulness are a very rare find

You push against this overwhelming passion
Hang on to logic as a safety vest
Yet, inescapably you're spelled into possession
Her silky image outshines the rest

Your mighty will directs your thoughts to working
Your boiling blood requests to feel her flesh
The flashing memories are ever so provoking
You get entangled in a lustful mesh

In every cell of your athletic body
Her shameless spirit found cozy home
Projecting images of her behaving naughty[a3]
It dips your days into seductive foam

Captivity that brings enormous pleasure
But seems so threatening for shaking your control
One of the kind encounter to treasure
Intensely beautiful and hot like fire ball

Leap off the cliff and spread your wings in freedom
Enjoy this epic and ecstatic ride
You're holding keys to gates of earthly Eden
Trust in the wind, relax, and simply glide!

Tip #2: Build Positive Association
Would you like to learn the secret to get your mate addicted to you? Make your partner associate you with pleasure, fun, care, and safety. When you

consistently aim to create a delightful experience with your lover, you both get to link enjoyment to each other's company.

Most couples do this naturally in the beginning of a relationship. Later, as familiarity grows, couples bring mundane things into the equation more and more. They stop planning surprises for each other and spending quality time together, and fall into a routine. In addition, life's problems, chores, and errands pile up. Consequently, the relationship loses its excitement and allure. While you cannot avoid life's challenges and responsibilities, you can direct the flow of your communication with your mate into a pleasurable realm.

Do you get turned on sexually when you speak of your past breakups, traffic, politics, and world problems? Those topics are stressful rather than arousing. Avoid them, especially during your first few dates, and in the long run. Whenever possible, don't get caught up in talking about work, a sick dog, or anything else potentially unpleasant. Have a solution-oriented focus, and don't discuss worrisome things more than absolutely necessary.

Seduction creates a mood for intimacy. It calls for a safe, enchanting, and sensual atmosphere, not only in your environment, but in your emotions. By reminding your lover and yourself to relax, open up and enjoy your time together, you are being of service to your relationship and to your mate. Chances are that you'll create hot memories, as well.

Build a sanctuary for your relationship, where you know you can find love, support, joy, laughter, and passion. Notice your lover's likes and do things to please him whenever you are inspired. When your mate showers you with affection and surprises, be a very gracious receiver and generously express your appreciation.

Keep your union sacred and delightful. Protect it from negativity and nurture it with creativity. Beautiful flowers don't grow without water, nutrients, and sunshine. The same is true for your love, it needs your care!

Tip #3: Maintain Novelty
Being predictable or too accessible is a turn off. Many heart-centered people try to be as honest as they can in a relationship. Honesty is admirable, but if you give a straightforward answer to every question, and people always know what to expect from you, it becomes boring. If a person is predictable, they become forgettable and disposable, because they stop creating emotional impact.

Imagine if you always drove 35 miles per hour. This would be safe and steady, but hardly exciting. On the other hand, driving like a racer all the time would be another extreme. It may get too stressful and not fun after a while. The combination is optimal. Your mate needs to feel safe in that they can rely on you and trust you, but at the same time, they want to be entertained, surprised, and thrilled.

Discover your edge and play with it! Give yourself permission to improvise, to be bold, and to do unexpected things. Dancing in a grocery aisle, or blowing soap bubbles in the office, taking your lover to skydive, or wearing a mask in the bedroom— allow your imagination to inspire you! Everyone has fantasies, so let yours come alive, and invite your partner to delight in your creativity and spontaneity.

You are a novelty! And novelty implies limited access. Have you noticed that words "limited edition" will cause you to pay attention? Most people take pride in owning one-of-a-kind things, or having unique experiences. Anything that's easily available, everywhere, at any time, is perceived as less valuable.

When you are in love, the desire to be with your beloved all the time is very tempting. Resist the urge, and avoid satiation. Most couples fall into this trap and become inseparable. This causes too much familiarity, takes the allure and mystery out of your relationship, and over time, neutralizes your polarity. Keep the hunger for each other acute. Spend time together and time apart. Even if you have been married for a long time and you love your spouse, don't spend all of your time with him. Have interests and friends outside of your marriage.

Imagine if you owned a restaurant. In order for your customers to enjoy their meals, they need to be hungry. The same is true for your relationship. If you want your lover to yearn for you and desire more time with you, you have to allow them to get hungry.

Charmed
You shook his hand and spun the wheel of fortune
His formal touch produced electric wave
Exchange of smiles and looks without caution
Induced obsessive encompassing crave[a4]

His eyes audaciously caressed your clothed body
His mind went boldly underneath your skirt
His fantasies of you were rather dirty
His words were colored in a daring flirt

His managed passion crumbled your defenses
His massive presence enveloped your soul
His sharp awareness disabled your pretenses
Your heart unlocked to his determined call

Like a silly moth enraptured by the fire
Ignoring all the hazards of pursuit
You made a choice to follow your desire
And taste the juice of the forbidden fruit

You danced in flames of sensual nirvana
You swam in ocean of euphoric blast
You saw eruptions of a huge volcano
And flew in mystic haze of silver dust

But morning came and took away this magic
Your dream dissolved like cloud in the sky
What's left is memory so achingly nostalgic
And a pair of wings that know how to fly

Remember, practicing the art of seduction will keep your love alive and flourishing. It will nurture your intimacy and connection. Have fun applying these tips! And if you would like to become a master, discover my Seductive Communication Program, which covers in detail the Rules and Elements of Seduction.

Love relationship is not a degree, where you earn a diploma and own it forever. It's a continuous invitation to step up, to grow, and to love deeper than a moment ago. It is an opportunity to explore the depths of your own heart and soul, and to see yourself in the mirror of your lover's eyes... Enjoy the reflection!

To get access to my three part video series— How to Stop the Power Struggle of Love and Start Feeling More Passion, Love, and Connection. Go to http://blisslifepress.com/conscious-love/bonuses/ now, to get immediate access to this training.

The Quest for Conscious Love: A Lesbian Perspective

Christine Dunn

"You will get exponentially more out of a conscious relationship than what you put into it. Choosing to walk this path will lead you to a deeper, more meaningful relationship both with yourself and with your partner. You'll discover a new richness in your relationship, a sustainable love, and more passion than you ever dreamed possible."
Christine Dunn

I never expected a casual meet up with a woman named Leah Love would completely transform how I thought about relationships and lead into a deeply meaningful co-creation of love.

Long before I met Leah, relationships and love had already taken center stage in my life. After struggling to make my first relationship work I decided to learn everything I could about communication, love, and building a strong partnership. In the late 90s there wasn't much lesbian specific relationship help out there. So I devoured everything I could find, gay or straight, and put it into practice in my life.

The Lesbian Love Guru
In 2011, after discovering the coaching industry and falling in love with it, I realized this would be the perfect way for me to share everything I'd learned over the years. I dubbed myself The Lesbian Love Guru and set up shop as a dating and relationship coach for lesbians. I was on a mission to help lesbians from around the world attract lasting love and create deeply connected, passionate relationships. I believed strongly that if you could just tweak a few things in your relationship the heavens would open, angels would sing, and you would forevermore live in the blissed out nirvana of the honeymoon phase. Not only did I believe this fairy tale, I was living it! I had an amazing ten year long relationship to prove it.

Anyone who met me and my first wife thought we were the perfect couple. We even thought we were the perfect couple and that we had this "love thing" figured out. We laughed at each other's jokes, held hands, were avid salsa dancers, and always seemed to be on the same page. She hid love notes in my desk and I never failed to buy her flowers on special occasions. We traveled the world together and I even surprised her with a dream vacation to Scotland for our 10th anniversary.

We lived our relationship on a simple premise— to be kind and loving to each other. And we did a great job living it. Friends of ours, on their wedding day, told us they modeled their relationship after ours and hoped to be as loving to each other. Everyone thought we had the perfect relationship. On the surface we were happy and "completed" each other a la Jerry Maguire (if you haven't seen it, it's a Tom Cruise/Renee Zellweger rom-com with a not so great message about needing another person to "complete" you).

Under the surface we were both deeply unhappy people. We had put so much stock in each other and the kind of partner each of us was "supposed" to be that we left little room for growth and evolution in our personal lives or in our relationship. We were stuck in the same patterns year after year— the same fights, the same compromises, and the same experiences. We both felt an uneasiness and discontent in our lives with no specific problem to point to or solve. We were stuck and no amount of Guru magic seemed to help us.

The End of an Era
Yes, that subtitle is dramatic! But for us, our friends, and family members our divorce felt earth-shattering. Our marriage seemed to crumble almost overnight leaving everyone in shock. The final catalyst for the break-up was just that— the final catalyst.

After fifteen years together we went our separate ways convinced that we couldn't break through the challenges that plagued our relationship for years.

As The Lesbian Love Guru I had to re-evaluate everything I'd been saying. Had I missed something in all of those books I read and workshops I attended? Was there some vital piece of information I missed that could have saved our relationship? Or, I wondered, "Is a fairy-tale, happily-ever-after relationship even possible?"

Disheartened and disillusioned I put my coaching practice on pause and decided to find the answers to my questions one way or another.

The Shift I Needed
What I know now is that we were tackling our problems from the wrong direction so no matter what we tried we would always fail. We had the best intentions, a deep love for each other and we were both totally committed to each other yet nothing we did worked. We needed a seismic shift in how we related to one another to propel us forward. But to learn this truth I had to step out of my comfort zone and completely transform how I thought about relationships.

When I met Leah Love I never expected her to turn my world so completely upside down. I began to question everything I thought about relationships from the very start. She introduced me to Tantra, sacred sexuality, and conscious love. Neither one of us had experienced a relationship where we could fully live these principles but we were eager to explore them together. We opened our hearts to each other and chose to rise into love, consciously, with our eyes wide open.

Conscious Love
In conscious love you are bringing your attention, intention, and presence to the relationship. You are committed to moving past unconscious patterns to live more fully in love and connection. The power of conscious love is life changing and can transform any relationship where both people are committed to embracing and expanding the love they share with each other.

Leah and I began our relationship journey together forging a new path into conscious love. Sometimes it was easy and sometimes it was so unbelievably difficult we almost gave up. But together we stuck to it. We wanted a deeply fulfilling, meaningful relationship that nourished both heart and soul.

I found the answers I was seeking when I left my first marriage. Not only could I create a more fulfilling relationship for myself but I also had new tools for helping others do the same. I re-committed myself to coaching full time and wrote a book with Leah called The Lesbian Intimacy Manual to teach others what we had learned.

Attracting the Love You Want
Whether you're in a relationship right now or not, the first shift towards experiencing more meaningful love in your life starts with you. As a companion to this chapter I've created a Conscious Love Attraction & Expansion Guide to help you customize your journey into more meaningful love. To download the guide visit the resources section of this book. If you are currently with a partner you may want to print out a copy for her to fill out too.

There are four keys to living and loving in a more meaningful way — responsibility, ownership, love, and evolution or R.O.L.E. for short. You can begin practicing these keys on your own and by doing so you will attract the love you want into your life.

Key #1 - Responsibility
You are responsible for making a shift in your life and in your relationship. If you want to have a more meaningful relationship you have to step up and decide to make it happen. You can't just wait for someone else to start the process for you.

With this first step it's important to take action to move forward. Decide on an action (no matter how minor) and take it now to begin transforming your love life into something more meaningful and fulfilling. Keep that momentum by taking another action and another. Actions may be simple like saying, "I'm sorry," when you make a mistake or they could be a bigger commitment like taking a meditation class to help you control your anger. Whatever your actions steps are, decide on one and get started!

Key #2 - Ownership
You need to own your emotions, triggers, patterns, beliefs, actions, and everything you say and do. Once you can take total ownership you leave the role of the victim and become empowered to make changes.

In my life I have had an emotional pattern of becoming extremely angry at my partners for minor problems. When I was angry I would find myself focusing on how my partner had wronged me and the changes they should make so I wouldn't feel so angry. I would feel victimized by their actions.

It was only through taking ownership over my anger that I was able to shift my emotional response. It empowered me to talk more clearly with my partner and ask to have my needs met in a more loving way. It also allowed me to see our conflicts from her perspective and own more of my role in our disagreements. When I could do that we were able to actually solve our problems rather than just shove them aside only to argue about them again in the future.

You must be willing to take ownership for your own stuff— all the feelings, beliefs, triggers, and patterns— if you want to shift your relationship into a higher state of conscious love.

Key #3 - Love
Love is not just a feeling in your heart that makes you all warm and fuzzy when you gaze into your lover's eyes. It's an action. Love is something you cultivate, share, grow, and shape. Love is in every kind word, every offer of forgiveness, every bowl of chicken soup brought to her when she's sick, and every act of empathy, compassion, or respect.

The most successful couples, the ones that have an ever deepening well of love for each other, didn't just stumble into the perfect relationship. They have learned the secret of loving each other through their actions and of growing that love year after year. They don't allow their love to wither away and die. They know love is a living and breathing organism that needs nourishment to thrive.

Nourish the love in your life starting with the love in your own heart. Feed it positive thoughts, share your love with those around you, and shape it into an unconditional love for others. Bring this love into your relationship and make it safe for your partner to open her heart up to you too.

Key #4 – Evolution
All relationships grow and change over the years. When you try to force your relationship to stay the same, it will grow stagnant or even become toxic. It's important to recognize the natural growth process of relationships and use this process to evolve your relationship into

something even deeper and more meaningful.

Journeying into conscious love will cause your relationship to evolve in new and exciting ways. For some this can feel scary, unfamiliar, or too vulnerable but it's important to allow the process to unfold. Do the work and trust that your relationship will continue to evolve to allow you both to experience deeper and deeper levels of conscious love.

Co-Creating the Relationship of Your Dreams
The R.O.L.E. model gives you the basic framework for creating a conscious relationship. As you may have noticed, each key depends on you as an individual choosing to experience your relationship differently than you may have in the past. If you are in a relationship right now, you both need to individually embrace all four keys and bring them into your relationship. By doing this you can co-create the relationship of your dreams.

Co-creation involves working together with a vision for the future you want to create. It's powerful because you are no longer drifting aimlessly. You no longer just "hope" things will change. Whether it's a more passionate sex life, more independence, or to welcome a new child into your family, you will begin facilitating change together in alignment with your highest good.

Leah and I believe in co-creating a relationship with a sacred sexual and spiritual side. We believe it is important to honor each other with special practices and to make spirituality a priority in our life. Before my last business trip I surprised her with a room full of candles, flowers, and sensual music. I led her to a chair in the center of the room where I had a small tub of water. I knelt in front of her, washed, and massaged her legs and feet while telling her all of the things I loved about her. It was a profound experience where we both felt deeply connected to each other.

Because we have consciously chosen to co-create a specific kind of relationship we both put our energies into the same shared vision. It helps us to shape the evolution of our relationship and we are continuously adding practices that are in alignment with it.

What Would You Like to Co-create?
Every couple should have a shared vision for their relationship. If you're single right now, create a vision for the kind of relationship you would like to be in. If you're in a relationship, sit down with your partner and talk with her about what is important to you both. Write your shared vision down and post it somewhere you can both read it regularly. Make sure to include your relationship values and goals. When it's time to make important decisions, review your shared vision and make sure the decision is in alignment with it.

Moving Deeper
Moving deeper into a more meaningful relationship can take many twists

and turns. Leah and I are learning to ride the waves and allow one another to grow and evolve along with the relationship. My ex-wife and I were unable to navigate the same uncertainty because we couldn't see the bigger picture. We were so committed to the particulars of our relationship that we stifled our own growth for years. It led to us both feeling varying degrees of unhappiness, depression, and anxiety.

Our relationship became locked into a certain framework early on. This is common for a lot of couples. My ex-wife and I became comfortable in our roles, communication style, sex life, and household habits and never made major changes to them even when they weren't working. We would tweak a little here or there and believe the problems to be fixed. Inevitably they never were and would spring up again and again. We didn't need one more Band-Aid for our problems. We needed a revolution.

Now when I work with coaching clients I no longer hand them a metaphorical box of Band-Aids for their problems. I give them a new way to connect with each other. I help them shake up their routine, re-evaluate their relationship vision or create one, and make lasting changes. I teach them about the R.O.L.E. model so they're empowered to co-create a stronger, more fulfilling relationship. With singles I help them prepare to attract partners that want to experience a more meaningful relationship. It's much easier to attract the right partner when you're aligned with the kind of love you want.

It's also much easier to practice the R.O.L.E. model outside of a relationship so you have the skills you need when you do find your Ms. Right.

Pam's Experience
One client came to me after spending seven years alone. Pam was ready to finally find the right woman for her and she knew she needed help breaking old patterns so she could create the best relationship of her life. Within a few months of working together she met and began dating a wonderful woman with a similar life path. They challenged each other to rise above their own limitations, be more authentic, vulnerable, and open than they ever thought possible. Together they stretched to create a conscious love partnership.

It was a joy to watch Pam and her partner co-create a relationship so extraordinary. Unfortunately most people will never come close to enjoying such a meaningful connection with another person either because they don't have the right tools or because the prospect of being so open is too scary for them. Pam was successful because she learned how to move from the usual relationship model into a conscious love model by using the right tools including R.O.L.E. and becoming totally committed to navigating through her own fears.

"Real love is an unconditional commitment to an imperfect

person."

Pam shared this quote (author unknown) with me and I wanted to share it with you here. Whether you're in a relationship right now and you want it to be more meaningful and fulfilling or you're single and looking for life changing love, the first place to start is with yourself. Find real love for yourself by making an unconditional commitment to an imperfect person—you! Practice conscious love by bringing your attention, intention, and presence to your relationship with yourself first then expand out to include others.

By starting with yourself first you'll discover an inner soul mate that will bring you peace and balance as you move into conscious love with a partner. People are often far harder on themselves than on others. Learning to love yourself first will make it easier to accept and embrace all aspects of a partner. To live in conscious love requires forgiveness, understanding, and humility. When we have that for ourselves it is far easier to give and receive it from others.

Your Path
As you expand to embrace a partner in conscious love remember that you are making an unconditional commitment to an imperfect person. You are committing to bringing your attention, intention, and presence to the relationship as well as moving past unconscious patterns to live more fully in love and connection. Conscious love will challenge you to take responsibility for creating the relationship you want, ownership over your own actions, beliefs, emotions, and unconscious patterns, expand your ability to love, and embrace growth and evolution.

Creating a more fulfilling, meaningful relationship will take some work on your part. I wish there was a Guru magic pill I could give you, I really do. But what I can promise is you will get exponentially more out of a conscious relationship than what you put into it. Choosing to walk this path will lead you to a deeper, more meaningful relationship both with yourself and with your partner. You'll discover a new richness in your relationship, a sustainable love, and more passion than you ever dreamed possible.

Through my relationship with Leah I feel I've been given the golden ticket to a more fulfilling life. I'm so lucky because not only do I get to experience a more meaningful relationship, but I also get to support clients who want to experience one too. I've learned in life the shortest path to success is modeling what other successful people have done. You don't have to re-invent the wheel. You can just follow the same path as those before you.

To help light your path, I've created a companion guide to this chapter called "The Quest for Conscious Love Attraction & Expansion Guide" to help you customize your journey into more meaningful love. Visit the http://blisslifepress.com/conscious-love/bonuses/. In the guide you'll discover exactly what you need to do experience a conscious love relationship in your life.

I wish you all the love in the world as you continue on your journey. Namaste.

Alchemy of Love:
Find the Key to keeping your Bank Account Flowing,
Your Body Glowing & Your Business Growing

Dr. Elena Estanol

"Love is the only power strong enough to heal our wounds,
deliver us from fear, create abundance, and bring us back to
our true brilliant selves. We simply need to start with self-love"
Dr. Elena Estanol.

"Open the door or I'll blow your mom's brains out!" shouted the gruff man's voice from the other side. My sister and I looked at each other and panicked.

"DO NOT OPEN THE DOOR! No matter what he says or does, do not open the door! Go upstairs!" We immediately heard these words from my mother.

My sister was quicker on her feet than I, so she ran up to call 911. But I was frozen to my spot, and listened through my tears, while I quietly looked through the peep-hole.

Gasp! I saw and heard my mother negotiating with the criminal, with a gun pressed against her head.

"Look … if you shoot me, you won't get anything but a warrant for your arrest and a guilty conscience...how about, I give you the keys to my car and you can take it with everything in it, and you promise me never to come back here again?"

Silence...

I heard my mother wrestling with her keys behind her back. I found out later that she was trying to unlink the car keys from the house keys and everything else.

"Okay, but hurry!" the man finally conceded.

My mother said, "Okay, you've got to lower the gun so I can look for them and you can get them..."

Suddenly, I heard the sound of sirens in the distance, growing louder as they got closer. Brilliant! This bought her enough time for the police to respond. The thief got scared and ran away, without the car.

I took one more look outside to be sure the thief was gone.

We rushed to open the door and hugged my mother. All three of us collapsed into a tearful embrace of relief.

I can't seem to remember how old I was, but in that moment, it was clear enough that we were incredibly lucky to be able to see and hug my mother again. We also understood once again, the frailty of life that we often take for granted.

Mexico City, where I grew up, has not been known for safety, yet I had never really experienced danger. We were not a rich family, but we lived comfortably. My parents had worked tirelessly to rise out of poverty, put themselves through school to become physicians and provide the best they could for us. However, it took me many, many years to unravel the effect that this experience had on me at a very subconscious level.

Most of us develop unconscious beliefs that drive our behaviors and our results, and they originate from experiences, teachings, and societal traditions that reinforce their validity and further embed them into our unconscious to become our individual TRUTHS.

This is just one such experience.

The underlying belief created by this experience was: "Having money is dangerous. It can cost you your life!"

This is just ONE neural-patterning laying the foundation, and a lifetime of experiences reinforced this synaptic connection. In simple terms, most of our learning happens by establishing synaptic pathways in our brain. The strength of these pathways gets reinforced every time we have similar experiences or others confirm that piece of knowledge.

Think of synaptic pathways as bike paths. We create bike paths through overgrown grass by riding our bike thousands of times until we create a path through grass. However, when we experience a traumatic event, these pathways get laid out chemically as if they were made with a laser beam. Only ONE round of a highly emotional experience is enough to create a pathway.

Can you think of "synaptic pathways" (emotional experiences) that have laid the foundation for well-established beliefs, emotional responses, and behavioral patterns for you?

Your relationship with money and food lays the foundation for the kind of the love life, and the kind of relationships you form in your life and in your business.

Intrigued? I will show you how these three seemingly disparate things have a common root and how the answer for more money, or freedom from food and your desire for conscious love is ONE and the same.

Peeling the onion
You may have picked up this book because you are interested in having a better relationship or to improve your sex life, yet the underlying beliefs that we develop as kids, and that are heavily reinforced by our society, hold the key to the relationships we have with money, with food, with love, with ourselves and others.

Before I came to understand this truth, I spent a lifetime trying to understand each of these things separately. Yet it is true, that our lives prepare us for our purpose, despite of the doubt that exists before it is truly in front of us, and we can look back and connect the dots.

As a PhD peak performance & counseling psychologist and intuitive prosperity & business mentor, I have spent thousands of hours listening to people's deepest struggles, fears, and greatest successes.

Being a psychologist and coach is a strange thing. It is a little bit like being a wise healer, health consultant, best friend, coach, cheerleader, confidante, confession priest, and the holder of ALL the secrets.

I get the honor of knowing people deeply and intimately in a way that few others get to see them in their lives. This has given me the amazing privilege of seeing the interconnectedness in things that many others consider to be completely different topics all together!

Being a highly intuitive, sensitive, passionate, empathetic and idealistic being didn't always feel like the best compilation of gifts. I have an innate ability to see what is beautiful in the world, and the innate potential that exists in people, places and ideas. However I am also highly sensitive to information that is all around me and often integrated into my impressions.

I always knew I wanted to make the world a better place, and I thought that being a ballerina was a great way to inspire and make people feel happy and provide relief from difficulties.

When I told my father I wanted to be a ballerina he replied, "If you do that you will end up living in a cardboard box!"

Have you ever experienced the pangs of finally expressing a deep desire from your heart, only to feel squashed or minimized? For me this was one experience that created a neural pathway.

Now of course, my dear father didn't intend to do this. He wanted to make sure I had a stable, secure and respectable job; just what every other parent wishes for their children.

However this interaction reinforced the "Societal Path" that we all get indoctrinated into pretty early in life: a path filled with a plethora of negative beliefs based on a system of scarcity. "Money doesn't grow on trees"; "You must work very hard for your money"; "You must earn your keep"; "You are not entitled to dinner until you have finished your chores"; "You must earn a place at the table"...

And on it goes... Can you add a few hundred more based on your experiences?

And what this does is that it sets us up in a journey in which ACHIEVEMENT, and DOING are not only THE most Prized thing, it is in Fact THE ONLY way to earn a respectable place in our world.

I want you to read this again. We have been indoctrinated to believe that: "Achievement IS the ONLY WAY to EARN A RESPECTABLE place in our world."

So your happiness depends on it, your remuneration depends on it, your safety depends on it, your very survival and right to exist and BE a human being depends on it!

So does it surprise you that we are the most stressed-out, medicated, depressed, anxious, sick, disconnected and addicted society with the highest divorce rate in the world?

We have this equation backwards. We have been indoctrinated to believe that the more we achieve, the more confident and worthwhile we will feel, which in turn it will lead to happiness and self-love. But the reality is that this keeps us locked in a never-ending hamster wheel in which we never feel we are good enough, where we don't ever appreciate our worth, love ourselves, or achieve true happiness. The reality is that everything happens in the reverse order. We must start with self-love, with happiness, and then everything else will follow.

Abundance vs Scarcity
As human beings we are neuro-biologically wired for connection. We develop attachments to people, and things, and these can be healthy or unhealthy attachments. The biological basis of these attachments is steeped in the synaptic pathways we build every time we have a particular experience and every time we have another experience to reinforce that

pathway.

We "suffer" every time we experience attachment to things we are unable to have. We suffer when we experience the pain associated with disappointment, grief, loss, disconnection, isolation, envy, despair, criticism and judgment among others. When we form beliefs that certain outcomes are responsible for our happiness, or connection, and these don't happen, we experience disappointment, sadness and suffering.

While there is no way to avoid pain, the experience of suffering is one we unconsciously "choose" in order to justify our feelings, our behaviors or actions. Suffering, allows us to stay in a victim mindset, where we can blame others, yet it also leads to disconnection. It becomes a catch 22. We feel abundance and connection when we experience love. We move into a scarcity mindset when we experience disconnection.

In fact, researchers have now identified that the early stages of romantic love is associated with dopamine pathways (responsible for happy feelings) in the reward system in our brains that regulate motivation, energy and focused attention.

Well, I am here to propose an integrative theory of what underlies so much of our suffering.

It is SCARCITY and JUDGMENT. The concept and belief of scarcity is what underlies EVERY inch of how we have been raised, how our world operates and why we struggle with money, food and love and everything else that unravels from these three associations. Judgment and criticism reinforce these beliefs and, serve as an ongoing measuring stick.

"Scarcity's job is to keep us in FEAR. Fear's job is to constrict our energies, our thoughts, our beliefs, our patterns and our actions." – Dr. Elena Estanol

The patterns and actions reinforced by fear will keep us locked up in an ever-shrinking box, making us smaller and smaller, until we disappear without a trace. Yes, it comes down to specific belief systems. However, these beliefs also have a corresponding activation in our amygdala, the part in our brain that creates emotions, feelings and sensations that reinforce these beliefs. This strengthens the pathway. Hence we learn by association.

Therefore, as we grow, we attempt to fit new information into "old boxes", old associations and beliefs that were created as children. So, for instance, if I had not done serious work in creating an alternate belief system around money, I would currently be struggling to make ends meet, having a difficult time trusting others, isolating in fear of being attacked in the event I had money, and very closed off to having any kind of fulfilling relationship. The fact that I have two very financially flowing conscious businesses, a beautiful romantic relationship, and many loving and collaborative friendships and business partnerships was only possible by upgrading this operating system.

If we stay blind to these processes, we are stuck living life with the operating system of a five, six or seven-year-old in a 30, 40, 50 or 70 year old body. We may not realize this is happening, as it is usually an unconscious process.

Without the upgrade, I may have continued to believe that having money was dangerous, and believed this was because there was not enough money to go around. This would reinforce a belief that there was a limited amount of that resource, (scarcity mindset) and therefore, it needed to be held onto as carefully as possible, and hidden from plain view so others wouldn't come to take it from me.

This pattern and belief also created an unconscious division; me vs others. This is the competition upon which our society is built. So if it is ME, I must win, or crush others so I can have; OR...if it is THEM, then they are taking it away from me. This is why this belief is SO DANGEROUS, and why I believe this is the root of many of our problems within ourselves, in our relationships, in our businesses and in our world.

When we operate from a scarcity mindset (not enough food, not enough money, not enough resources, not enough love), we contract, we close ourselves to receive, or we hoard it and stop the energy flow. And all of this comes from an underlying lack of deep, unabashed, full and expansive LOVE for ourselves.

Where the wallet and plate meet Food.

Not surprisingly, this pattern also underlies our relationship with food as well. Have you noticed the speed at which you eat?

How do you think about food? Do you restrict yourself? Do you show rebelliousness through food? Do you hoard it? Do you waste it?

Do you hurry up and dish up before others come and leave you without any? Or do you wait for others to dish up before you dish your own? Do you give up your food to give to someone else, or do you share it?

Have you noticed that women often "compete" in regards to food, to see who eats the healthiest plate, who will eat the most? Who will have dessert?

Why Do We Do This?
Simple! It comes from a place of unworthiness, and all our behaviors are veiled attempts to make ourselves feel better.

In my own life, my desire to please, be accepted, and loved, put me in a path towards achievement.

For one, my father is a brilliant neurologist, prize-winning author, and self-taught musician. My mother is an incredible ophthalmologist, teacher, painter and life-long learner. They are amazing people who have accomplished more than many human beings and who have spent their life doing, creating and working very hard. As a sensitive being, I caught on quite soon, that the path to love, acceptance and attention was through achievement. So I threw myself into this path. This was strongly reinforced by society.

The problem was that I was not doing this because I felt aligned with my purpose or my passion, as I am now. Much of it was in clear rebelliousness, and some of it was simply to prove a point, and make myself feel better, smarter and more worthwhile.

Judgement and Criticism
However, nothing seemed good enough; there was always someone that was a better dancer, that got a better role, someone that understood concepts better, got better grades, got to speak more...and so I fell into the trap of unworthiness, and for me, this came in the form of an eating disorder.

Now if you don't know about eating disorders, they are incredibly complex and dangerous diseases that claim more young lives than any other psychiatric condition. They are gravely misunderstood, and, as it is common in our human wiring, we often separate ourselves by saying, "I am not one of THOSE people"... but the reality, having been one of these people, it is not something we wish, something we purposefully do to garner attention or love. It is simply a manifestation of the unworthiness, the judgment, and the criticism that we hold towards ourselves.

However, they highlight the patterns that we all have, in the extreme. People with eating disorders become obsessed with food, cooking, and ingredients. Often they restrict themselves, yet hoard food for "later" (as if there was a famine), and other times, they eat compulsively, quickly, before anyone else can notice them. Often in an attempt to numb their feelings, yet again, the eating disorder thrives on judgment, criticism and control. It is antithetical to love.

Having recovered from this horrific disease, our wellness center, Synapse Counseling has specialized in treating young adults and families who struggle with eating disorders for the last 15 years. These are extreme representations of the disconnection that happens when we abandon ourselves, when we live in constant criticism and comparison, and when no matter what we do, or how we are in the world, we judge ourselves to be "not good enough".

So the next time you notice yourself saying that you were "bad" because you ate dessert, or that you were "good" because you had salad, think about how this is part of this pattern of judgment that keeps us in a loop destined for self-criticism and hatred, that we later project and reflect onto those around us.

"The damage that self-judgment and self-criticism cause is deep, insidious and thwarts our growth and highest potential."
– Dr. Elena Estanol

And what is fascinating is that though eating disorders may be extreme examples, everyone has experienced this feeling to one degree or another. It simply shows up in different ways: addictions, drugs, alcohol, cigarettes, video games, sex, TV, money or work. It doesn't really matter, because what is underneath this is a disconnection from our true selves, from our true source and from our true essence.

Money

I once worked with a very bright fourteen-year-old, and she came in once and said, "I am noticing that I am obsessing about money. I keep counting money, and worrying about how we are going to come up with all the money for school, etc."

I simply asked her, "Where do you think this is coming from?" and her answer floored me: "Oh! It is my eating disorder! Masquerading as something else, but it is the same thing. I am obsessing about something that doesn't exist

"Wow!"

I wish that many of my heart-centered entrepreneurs would see this too. As my counseling and wellness practice evolved, grew and was thriving, I got more and more people asking me how I built the center I did, especially since we do not bill insurance.

As I began talking with my colleagues, I realized there was a great wound, a great divide in most healers' minds and spirits. I realized that many of us have struggled with the concepts of marketing, selling, and receiving money. Yes, we may want it, but most healers just want it to appear in their bank account, they generally don't want to talk about it, or "handle it", and most of the time, what I hear is that they just want "enough to pay the bills". This is sad.

For example, I was at a friendly gathering of therapists and healers, when we decided we would play poker. I got excited as this is one of my favorite games to play. Many said they didn't know how to play so I happily taught the game. But what transpired next caused my jaw to drop to the floor, and I had to think quick on my feet before the drool started to come out.

As I was mentioning the value to assign to each chip, I said, "this black chip is 500"...I heard a chorus of people saying... "Wow, that is too much! Can we make it 5?"...what? How about the 100s and the 25s... They wouldn't have it. So we played a game with chips that were worth 25 cents, $1 and $5. Mind you, the actual money they had to put into the pot to play was the same.

But the idea of "betting" with these high numbers was too uncomfortable.

What this experience made abundantly clear is that there is a huge disconnection and wound for many healers, therapists, holistic practitioners, and other heart-based entrepreneurs around RECEIVING MONEY!

And this became the motivation for my coaching business, Luminescent Life. I saw there were many amazing healers, coaches, therapists, counselors, holistic practitioners, teachers, speakers, writers and creatives that could bring amazing light to the world, that were not doing so, because they were getting burnt-out, sick, and frustrated, and eventually unable to care for others as well, because their own needs were not being met. I also decided that we are capable of changing the business-as-usual landscape, and create businesses with love at the center, where we create win/win relationships, and philanthropic partnerships.

Money is uncomfortable. Most don't even want to talk about it, say the word, or have to deal with it. So how in the world do you plan to have a real business that makes a profit?

I since realized how this was also part of our societal imprinting and web of beliefs. We come from a long tradition that has many beliefs about spirituality, healing, and arts, in which these professions and professionals are not well-compensated for their gifts.

Can you think of some of these?

"Starving Artists", "Begging Priests", "Money is dirty, hence it cannot be associated with spirituality or healing", "Sliding-scale services", "taking care of the poor".

I believe this is partly due to the high degree of empathy we have. For instance, as a child, I was a picky eater and so was my sister. In an attempt to help us eat and appreciate our food, our parents placed pictures of starving children in Africa in the wall we faced while we ate. It was a simple motivational strategy. Right? Well, in my mind, this is what happened:

"Oh those poor children, if they don't have enough to eat, then I shouldn't eat either; why should I have food and not them?"

So needless to say it backfired on my parents. It didn't cross my mind that depriving myself of food didn't actually give food back to those in need. It just punished me and those around me. I have seen this pattern replay over and over with thousands of clients. It is just a form of self-hatred and self-punishment. Can you relate to any of it?

I use this as an example, because I believe it is the same with money. If we live from a scarcity place, then if we have something (food, money, or love) then it means we are "taking it away" from someone else so we can have it. And it actually closes us up, decreases our vibration and attracts more scarcity. In fact, even our language in business, in regards to philanthropic ventures, we tend to say "give back", which actually assumes we "are taking something away", instead of "paying forward" for example.

Money is simply a magnifier of what is already there. What I mean by this is that money is a neutral energy that simply enhances and magnifies the values, and the intentions in our hearts and in our beings. Though we have often associated "money and power" with negative things, as we have seen our share of individuals with money and power take advantage of others, it wasn't necessarily money or power that corrupted them. Corruption was already there. Money and power simply allowed them to make it more prominent and their impact reverberate deeply. So if you have a pure, clean, and loving heart, imagine what you might be capable of creating in the world if you had more money and power to magnify the goodness that already exists within you?

The fire to work with coaches, healers, counselors and heart-based entrepreneurs burned deeper once I realized some of the most loving, empathic and light-bearing beings in our world, are being crushed and drowned out because of this wound and inability to receive. What would our world be like if the people that had the most power and money, were the people that had the purest hearts, the most love and light to spread in the world? Being open to receiving money and living in abundance creates more of that abundance. The more we live in abundance, the more we create it around us. This can truly revolutionize our world.

An experience working with one of my business clients illustrates this. We were creating a strategy to build her business, and I listened to her passions, desires and ways to create and impact the world, she was completely lit up and excited, her energy was expansive and tingly.

When I asked her about her financial goals and how we would align these two, she slumped down and sighed. It became apparent she had a huge internal conflict about receiving money and allowing this abundance to flow in her life. So she unconsciously did things that sabotaged her progress and kept her not just from having the financial freedom she consciously desired, but also from the expansive impact she is meant to have in the world. And this was heartbreaking to see!

We did some work around clearing some of these blocks and aligning her passion, her purpose, and her strategy in LOVE, and all of a sudden everything just fell into place for her as she created a life of love, service and abundance. If you are interested in receiving my "Rewiring Prosperity Guide and 4-Part Course to Clear Your Most Common Money blocks. Go Here http://blisslifepress.com/conscious-love/bonuses/

So, consider this...if you are not open to receiving the bounty and abundance of food and money in a healthy way... if you are not able to care for your body from a place of love, and generate a profit from a place of gratitude, how will you create, and engage in a conscious romantic relationship in which you open yourself up to receiving, where you give without keeping tabs, and where you love without suffocating the other person?

How will you create a business in which you create meaningful relationships and partnerships that are profitable and fun?

The Journey to Wholeness
Well, the truth is that we have been doing the best we could, given the information we were given. Yet this westernized perspective of achieving and getting things so we can be happier, feel better, get the guy, get the girl, have the "ideal" life has us running in a never ending cycle that has become a tailspin.

Our parents, grandparents and ancestors didn't mean to hurt us; they were imparting their best wisdom based on their experience. They had lived through several wars, the depression and many market crashes. Having a scarcity perspective and an achievement mindset is what got THEM ahead, so they wanted to impart their best wisdom.

Fortunately, WE are a new version of humanity. We are evolving into the intuition and transformation age, and continuing to do things in this manner has everything we wanted to avoid.

We must switch our paradigm from achieving, to giving and receiving.

From Competition to Collaboration.
FROM SEPARATENESS (OR SPECIALNESS) TO CONNECTION AND LOVE.

And the simple change that can be extremely difficult to practice; Self-Love.

Love Wins!

What we need is SELF-LOVE.

"I truly believe that self-love holds the keys to health, happiness, success, love, conscious, fulfilling relationships and world peace." –Dr. Elena Estanol

Self-love is the simple act of coming back to ourselves, of embracing our true nature and of honoring ourselves in taking care of ourselves, asking for help and being open to receiving... It is connecting with our Divine Feminine energy in a receptive and compassionate manner.

Fear constricts and love expands. This is my core philosophy. When we live from scarcity we are in a perpetual contracted state. It is hard to give and it is very hard to receive. You are armored up, blocked up and walled in! Even if things were flowing to you, you would not even notice!

It is so sad to see how self-judgment and self-criticism have become permanent fixtures in our internal landscape, and how in turn this reflects in the external landscape of our actions, our relationships and the way that we show up in the world.

We are ALL love, luminous and brilliant beings, with unique gifts we bring the world.

As kids we are all fascinating, curious and genuine. Through school we learn that being "different" is bad and we spend the rest of our years attempting to blend in, fit into a mold of "normalcy and mediocrity" and ultimately disconnect from our true essence: "love".

"Love is all there is!" Once you drop your ego, once you drop the pretenses, once you drop the self-criticism, and self-judgment you will see that this is who and what we are."

Learning to reconnect to love and cultivate self-love is a crucial step to healing our bodies, our minds, our hearts and our spirits.

Ultimately, self-love is at the core, the foundation of healing our relationship with food, welcoming abundance and prosperity, having healthy romantic relationships, and creating win/win relationships in our businesses that make a meaningful difference in our world. We can create the world we want to live in through our businesses, through our relationships, and it all starts with self-love and the relationship you create with yourself. Ultimately, the relationship we have with ourselves is the longest-standing relationship we will ever have. The quality of this relationship sets a pattern by which every other relationship is mirrored and projected into the world.

I can't finish this chapter without speaking about compassion and how I view the intersection of the most important elements in creating conscious relationships and peace.

Compassion
Compassion is at the root of any healing relationship. It has been defined
as the emotional response we have when perceiving suffering in others
that elicits an authentic desire to help. Compassion is a primary
characteristic of attachment and we are wired for it, yet society often
short-circuits our ability to practice compassion towards ourselves and
others. The more we have experienced difficult or painful experiences, and
the more we have interpreted them as "bad", the more we have erected
walls, gotten hardened, or shut down our hearts, the less compassionate
we become.

When we disconnect, we disconnect from compassion and love; we
disconnect from our true selves. These two are intrinsically interconnected
because they are "heart openers" as we call them. However these two
emotional pathways involve the brain's motivation and reward circuits
(these are the pathways in charge of producing an 'internal' reward, such
as feeling happy, excited, or cuddly). They provide our capacity to self-
regulate our emotions, reduce stress, improve our health and aid in
survival. But more than anything they underpin our emotional
attachments, and our relational wiring.

Compassion allows us to embrace another's suffering with love, support,
and kindness. Our brains are equipped with, what scientists have called:
"mirror neurons". These neurons are believed to function as a tuning fork
of sorts. They are basically capable of vibrating at the same frequency as
that of what they are experiencing. So if you happen to associate with
successful, high level entrepreneurs, who are taking great risks and
creating amazing results, and you hear them, watch them, and surround
yourself with them, as is the case with my ELEVATE mastermind, then
your brain begins vibrating at that level and creating neural pathways that
are based on success! It is really quite miraculous. And these neurons are
what can detect what another person may be feeling, or experiencing.
Recognizing that we need to practice compassion, not just for our fellow
human beings, but that we need to start with ourselves, is of primary
importance. I believe that our painful experiences and suffering provide an
opportunity for us to attune to the pain and suffering that others
experience, and if we can turn that inward, then we continue to expand
this capacity.

For instance, I used to be somewhat critical of people who "fell apart" after
a break-up. I was not too patient or kind. Then life happened. I had a
terrible break-up and had my heart handed to me. Then I was able to
experience first-hand the true pain that comes from the disconnection, and
the grief that ensues following a break-up. Since then, I have the utmost
amount of respect and compassion for anyone going through this heartbreaking experience.

When we are able to practice being kind and compassionate towards
ourselves, especially when we are in pain, hurting, and especially if we

have made a mistake, we are in fact EXPANDING OUR CAPACITY FOR LOVE. This is not just love towards ourselves but towards others as well because we simply reflect back to others how we feel about ourselves.

In my opinion, compassion is one of the prerequisites for conscious relationships, conscious businesses and peace. Below you will find a diagram of how I view the intersection of these three important concepts: Self-love, Compassion and Abundance and how these intersect to create peace, prosperity, philanthropy and conscious love.

CONSCIOUS LOVE DIAGRAM

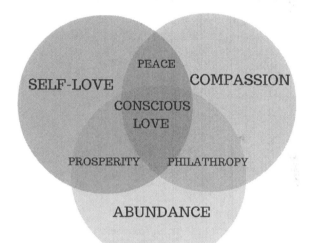

Dr. Elena Estanol Ph.D., M.F.A.

In search of Conscious love?
If you are feeling stuck, and disconnected, check your relationship with yourself. Are you loving or critical? Are you judgmental and demanding? Or are you kind and compassionate?

Self-love is a foundational practice from which so much of our growth evolves. Increased focus, passion, purpose, productivity, profits, abundance, health and success all stem and grow with self-love. Conscious love is about our recognition that deep inside, we are all one and the same. We are wired to mirror and connect through love, and recognize that we are all brothers and sisters meant to live in love, harmony and peace.

It's not to say it is the only practice you need, but rather it is a foundational practice that if left unchecked will have you spinning your wheels doing ALL KINDS OF THINGS and not seeing the results that you desire. This is ONE important piece.

When abundance, self-love and compassion meet, we get conscious love. When self-love and abundance meet, we receive prosperity, and when we have abundance and compassion, we are able to share the love and abundance with those in need through philanthropy. I wanted to share the overall tenets with you, so you can also become a beacon of love and light.

So...

If you have been worried about losing weight, stressing about making money, achieving the next challenge, making the deal, or getting the ideal body from a critical and judgment laden way, then don't be surprised if you are having trouble finding Mr. or Mrs. Right.

We can't open ourselves to true love, until we have learned to love ourselves deeply and fully. This occurs when we have realized we are valuable because of who we are and not what we do or accomplish. You will find that as you love yourself, you elevate your vibration, and you expand your energy. Now your opportunities to welcome and receive money and love and conscious collaborations will multiply before your very eyes!

"Love expands everything it touches,
while fear constricts everything in its path.
Embrace your ability to create powerfully in your life,
by choosing love."
- Dr. Elena Estanol

Publisher's Bio

Christopher Sherrod

Christopher Sherrod is a conscious entrepreneur with long hair who loves to meditate. He believes business has to be transformed through telling the truth and shaking things up. Business owners and soul-based leaders all over the world seek out Chris for his unique take on how conscious, creative entrepreneurship cannot only add to their bottom line, but change the world at the same time. He is the co-owner of BlissLife Publishing, helping creative entrepreneurs to launch their books through his paradigm-shifting strategic philanthropy publishing system.

Known as a multiple bestselling author and a prolific creative entrepreneur, Chris has been profiled, quoted or reviewed in dozens of publications including: Good Men Project, Medium, Fox Small Business, CNN radio. When he's not launching new businesses or helping authors get published, he can be found playing and producing music or walking on sunset beaches with his long-time partner Nan. BlissLifePress.com.

Nan Akasha

Nan Akasha is a born innovator, leading an emerging global 'Conscious Business' movement to transform lives through adding "Profitable Philanthropy to business". Co-founder of the award winning publishing house, BlissLife Press, Nan helps transformational authors start a movement, build a tribe and combine purpose and philanthropy to create healthy profits while raising money for charity at the same time. Featured in "Fast Company" magazine, Nan combines 30 years experience of building six and seven Figure business with her intuitive and wealth creating gifts.

Author of seven #1 bestselling books, and 133 audio programs, Nan speaks, leads retreats and travels worldwide to spread her message of peace, partnership and prosperity.

Nan is known as the "Secret Weapon" for finding and living your Soul's purpose, and she has an "uncanny ability to get to the heart of what stops you".

Committed to consciously evolve the way business is done, Nan is a Conscious Business Consultant, and speaks on how to add "Profitable Philanthropy" to your business and increase your cashflow dramatically. Pioneering a new way to do business that makes good while doing good, BlissLife Press has created the World's first 'Profitable Philanthropy Book Launch". Helping authors, creative visionaries, and Conscious Entrepreneurs to get their message out with massive impact, influence and income.

Nan is a passionate writer. Her own books include "Be Love", "Already Rich: Secrets to Master Your Money Mind", "Thoth Book of Magic. A Daily

Manual to Manifest the Life Your Soul Intended" and the upcoming "Conscious Business Principles: Creating a Business of Higher Purpose and Profits.", and her new line of "Bliss Bites" - small profound, beautiful artistic books. An Artist, and Spiritual Teacher, Nan's programs like the international hit "Flip Your Rich Switch", and the "Live Your Purpose & Fulfill Your Fully Funded Mission" and "Soul Channeling & FreeFlow Writing", are highly experiential for deep, lasting transformation.

Nan's Sacred light body work transcends healing and opens your Life Purpose Blueprint. Her sacred retreats, and life changing writing experiences, free you to live the life your Soul intended.

Clients and colleagues worldwide call Nan their "Fairy Godmother"... of transformation, and money, and love. She lives an enchanted life in San Diego with her Soulmate Chris, and her beloved twins on a college adventure. BlissLifePress.com and NanAkasha.com.

Meet The Love Experts

Alain Torres

Alain Torres guides world-renowned Power Couples™ and Power Players™ to systematically get on the same page and stop holding each other back. He helps them reignite their fire so they achieve their big mission and bridge the gap to become the ultimate team that does extraordinary things in the world.

In his coaching practice, Alain reveals the specific areas of imbalance that cause instability and a lack of understanding. His in depth knowledge and personal experience lays the foundation that gives you the confidence to know once and for all that you can succeed even though you feel like you're going in opposite directions. For the past ten years he's helped powerhouses to stop tiptoeing around their relationship - so they can stand in their power and get back the excitement and fun they experienced when they were inseparable.

Are you ready to grow into the Power Couple™ you always knew was possible? It's empowering to have a proven system to get you on the same team. After all, your strategy hasn't been giving you the results you set out to achieve. You don't have to keep banging your head against a wall - it's time to stop struggling and get to the bottom of this. Today's the day you choose your relationship fate.

Lana Shay

It was 39 minutes before the performance at the National Miss American Coed Pageant, and her stomach rejected breakfast. While hugging the toilet, Lana confessed to her mother that she was too nervous to perform. This moment was a clear indication that Lana wasn't destined to take a conventional route to the stage.

Two decades later she took on a more fitting role as a body paint model, and was internationally recognized in just one year. Armed with over twelve years of dance and yoga training, she appeared on GSNTV's Skin Wars, with professional contortionists. Months earlier, she appeared on the stage of the Pantages Theatre in Hollywood, as a contestant of the notorious series, America's Got Talent. Lana has now been featured on ABC News, Business Insider, MSN, The Huffington Post, New York Daily News and numerous other international publications.

While the limelight was on, Lana was balancing another act. Literally. In 7 inch stilettos. Lana graced gentleman's clubs across America for 9 years as an exotic dancer, eventually taking on the stripper mecca of Las Vegas. Meeting with so many personalities in this intimate environment, she pretty much earned a Master's in Psychology (minoring in Male Psyche) via the school of life experience—building a constructive rapport with a host of diverse clientele.

Physical and mental exhaust eventually resulted from what felt like a marathon performance. Lana was confronted with the despair of living inauthentically. She sat down to dinner with close friends, one being Mina Shah; former Peak Performance Strategist for world-renowned life coach Anthony Robbins. Mina offered Lana a stern reality check, and asked "Why aren't you teaching people about health?!" Noting that this was Lana's deepest passion and expertise.

The "Sensual Foodist," was birthed through decades of emotional struggle, as Lana faced her closest friends and family suffering with cancer and other life-threatening conditions. She has lived her life determined to break the cycle of disease and dysfunctional relationships in her family. Lana advocates sustainable practices in the kitchen, with sensual AKA real food, as a catalyst for igniting the senses and a conscious relationship. She advises fully experiencing the pleasure of life in the human form, while encouraging couples, and aspirants alike to embrace a passion for living a conscious lifestyle. She proudly attributes her skill of keeping the kitchen fun, sexy and flirty to years of perfecting the art in stilettos.

A few of Lana's current endeavors include private sensual kitchen workshops, finding a way to end the manufacturing of plastic products, Recovery Coaching, and experiencing new paths to sensual pleasure through food, to share with fellow pleasure seekers.

Deborah Morehead

Think you have relationship issues? How about being stood up on your 30th birthday by your drug addicted boyfriend and chasing him down at a local bar. In the past, Deborah settled for SUCKY relationships. The last straw was when her boyfriend stole the VCR for drug money (the one she had borrowed from her father).

Deborah knew relationships didn't have to be like this. She struggled for years being in relationships the only way she knew how, repeating the same painful patterns. She was determined to figure out this relationship stuff. And, she did. Now, Deborah is an international highly trained leader, expert therapist and successful teacher with more than 20 years of expertise in the business of helping people.

It doesn't have to take years for you to go from embarrassingly sucky to amazingly wow relationships. For Deborah it took moving to another state, a master's degree, a new career as a therapist and some of her own personal therapy to bring relationship freedom into her life.

As a woman of passion and purpose. She knows that people can start living a life of freedom, a life that can be truly abundant and full of joy when it comes to relationships. She is living proof herself and now with ease and speed helps people reach this place in their lives too.

Deborah uses her unique gift of looking right into your heart, knowing you almost better than you know yourself, recognizing your core needs and helping you transform yourself and your relationships into a life you truly desire.

As Vice President of one of Los Angeles County's largest non-profit mental health agencies Deborah gained strengths and expertise working with some of the most vulnerable clients in LA County. For fifteen years she administered various programs working directly with severely mentally ill youth, and their families, who were placed in foster care all while maintaining a thriving private practice as a therapist.

A teacher at heart Deborah has taught Marriage Family Courses at University of Phoenix as well as teaching elementary and middle school. Continuing her love of teaching, she developed and lead diverse workshops and trainings for clients and company staff. She has presented at national conferences and participated in and co-chaired countywide committees to improve county practices.

Deborah has appeared on local NBC, CBS and Fox stations numerous times regarding her extensive work on creating the life and relationship you truly desire.

Hopefully you weren't chasing someone down on your 30th birthday but whatever sabotaging and painful relationships you find yourself in – YOU DON'T HAVE TO STAY THERE! You don't have to struggle in your relationships. You have the power to change your life and relationships. Join Deborah and her extraordinary Happy Relationship Success System to help you get your very own Amazingly Wow Relationships.

Christopher Menné

Chris Menné's passion is joining the energies of transcendent sexuality with higher-consciousness to support healing, growth and awakening. Committed to serving the higher-consciousness which is emerging in the world today, Chris left an established career as an airline pilot, and immersed himself in graduate studies of Psychology, Consciousness, and Spirituality, eventually receiving an MA in Transpersonal Psychology. Drawing upon 20 years of life experience with many personal growth and transformational modalities, and dedicated to a high standard of professional delivery, Chris applies his graduate work in direct teachings, coaching and counseling, supporting individuals on their path of personal development, embracing higher-consciousness and spiritual growth.

Chris' more focused work with sexuality and consciousness became a clear calling when he saw the widespread challenges many people experience in their intimate relationships, once they had committed to a path of personal development or spiritual growth. This focused work was further illuminated, as Chris experienced his own breakthrough in an intimate relationship. The core shift was seeing, then choosing to relate less from an egoic or relative sense of of self, and more from Presence or a higher sense of self.

As many "on the path" can attest, this is easier said than done. To really access and apply Presence, Chris and his partner took on challenges in their relationship that became points of empowerment, calls to action to become more conscious within their relationship. Utilizing the powerful root energies of sexuality which drive erotic and pleasurable sensations to more deeply awaken and stabilize a core sense of self, or Presence, Chris and his partner's real breakthrough occurred as they both continued to work on embodying Presence in the midst of greater and greater challenges. Able to experience one another, more from a place of Presence, and less from a relative or egoic sense of self, even when in the midst of conflict, was the key. Chris and his partner could clearly see that they had tapped into something profound, utilizing sexuality as a resource to support authentic mature love from a higher source, which promoted durable, spiritual awakening, regardless of the outcome of the relationship...

Although this higher experience of sexuality does require intention and attention to cultivate; it yields huge benefits such as; healing past wounds, supporting higher functioning in life, and authentic spiritual awakening. This natural, higher experience of sexuality, which is approached through practices like meditation or yoga, becomes part of one's overall sexual expression. Every aspect of sex and sexuality, ranging from the erotic, to relaxed and playful sex, to romantic lovemaking, all become more enriched. We open to a fascinating lifetime path of clarifying perception, which increasingly reveals that Presence experiences and perceives, while ego only interprets, and; we truly begin to "see" ourselves and another. As we wake up, we find ourselves on an unparalleled life-giving path, with the ability to experience sex, love, self and others, from a higher source.

Single or coupled, Chris supports individuals in embodying this core intelligence of their sexuality and higher consciousness, and through this embodiment, how to connect with and relate to that same core intelligence in another, both when meeting someone new, or when partnered. This is an empowered life path of creating highly conscious and profoundly satisfying sexual-love relationships, a path which Chris engages in enthusiastically, and with steady competence.

Chris is a Co-Author of the #1, International Bestselling book, Conscious Love: Enlightened Relationships and Soulful Sex.

Lucia Nicola Evans

Lucia is in tune with Universal Truth and Harmony. She brings Presence, Depth, Love and Playfulness wherever she goes. She is passionate about love and empowering others to love more. She radiates Authenticity and enjoys expressing her True Self in a variety of creative and innovative ways. Lucia takes time to feel into things. She listens deeply from her heart and acts from her inner guidance where she is able to make decisions that are in alignment with her inner knowing.

Lucia's healing has been a journey of deep soul discovery and mind training. The challenge in her early years reached a peak with the diagnosis of Juvenile Rheumatoid Arthritis at the age of 14. Over more than a decade through her determination, perseverance and belief in herself, Lucia was able to heal herself. Because conventional cures were ineffective, Lucia was led to alternative ways of healing. She learned that she needed to listen to her own authority for the cure. In order to accomplish this, she went on a journey of self discovery, where she turned inward to get in touch with the source. She discovered the core issue - lack of self-love, acceptance and self-expression.

As an Empath and an Intuitive, Lucia feels intensely. Due to her past frustrations around not knowing how to express how she truly felt, Lucia learned effective heart centered communications skills. She has not only realized how to communicate from her heart, she now knows how to differentiate her feelings from those around her. She has developed awareness to embrace feelings on a wide spectrum, from despair and fear, to love and bliss. As a result, it is safe for her to voice her true feelings.

With her acute awareness and empathic skills, Lucia has learned how to hold a safe space for others to explore the depth of their suppressed feelings using the Power of Authentic Relating. She knows Authentic Relating is vital for our growth as individuals, and as a species - keeping us in touch with what is real.

Lucia has guided many people and continues to guide people through their own healing process. She is gifted at seeing each person from a Holistic perspective. As an author in the book, "Conscious Love", Lucia shares how living Conscious Love is so important. By holding a space of presence for people to become aware in how they Relate, there is more opportunity to live Conscious Love. Lucia has always been interested in bringing more truth, inspiration and love to the world. She has committed her whole life to understanding relationship dynamics. Lucia practices the Ancient Art of Aikido, to help her harness her power. Aikido goes beyond resolving physical conflict, into the experience and embodiment of Harmonizing Universal Love. What makes Lucia feel happy and fulfilled in her relationships is being present, listening from her heart, and making time for Authentic Relating. As a Relationship Alchemist and Spirit Guide, she facilitates healing circles in Vista California and does presentations on the Journey of Self Love.

Lucia was born in England and moved to the US in 1992. She has a BA in Psychology and is a Certified Massage Therapist. With more than 15 years of experience in the healing profession, practicing massage, coaching, and through deep self-inquiry, Lucia has the hands-on experience, wisdom and insight to follow your thread of consciousness in order to get to the root cause of each imbalance in your system.

Kristina Shumilova

"I Stand for Love"
Despite following her pursuit of happiness, at the age of 27, Kristina found herself questioning life, failing a marriage, and going through a divorce. Realizing she needed to change within, and not finding what she needed from conventional relationship counseling, Kristina forged her own path to love and fulfillment.

#1 International Best-Selling Author of "Conscious Love" and the new "Get over Your Ex in a Week" and "Cultivating Self Love" programs and books, she now coaches men and women all over the world in emotional health and well-being.

Kristina believes that letting go of the past, healing or getting over "it" doesn't have to be hard or isolating but instead can be empowering. Her passion and work isn't about giving love or relationship advice. Kristina's mission is to help you reset your love buttons and re-create love, no matter what the circumstances. For you to be your own hero or heroine that doesn't give up or give in but stays true to their heart.

"Kristina is wise beyond her years and her style of coaching is natural and deeply intuitive. Her insights, guidance and gift are invaluable." – Diane McDonald, Founder of A Woman Alive

Kristina was born and raised in Siberia, Russia, and today you can catch her enjoying life in California.

Deborah Nielsen

Deborah Nielsen is a pain navigator, hope builder and love facilitator; empowering her clients to find their core self. In both the Dance of Love and the Dance of Life, Deborah invites those who work with her to practice more compassion for themselves and the people they love. She encourages infusing conscious compassion into all relationships, and utilizing one's inner compass of intuition and insight. This is the groundwork for enjoying the dance of communication, gradually incorporating, melding and merging, more compassion and insight, which can deepen intimacy and build resilience and contentment within the dynamic Dance of Love. We co-create this Dance of Life in conscious, loving practice.

Deborah sees through the lens of wholeness, core character and purpose. As a survivor, herself, she has moved through trauma, to greater peace, purpose and passion., She believes that even if we feel broken, we can restore and build resilience and greater wholeness. Recognizing that, 'you are more than your experience, more than your pain,' Deborah guides her clients to dive deep into their pain in order to remove obstacles. When her clients resurface, and redefine their purpose, they are able to live with more peace and passion. They are stronger, clearer and more empowered, and are better able to hold love for self and others. From this place of clarity, they can begin to create sustainable, collaborative, love partnerships.

Deborah's children, now grown men, have been an inspiration and a source of pride and joy in her life. She has found her true match, love partner. Together they love to dance and hike. In both her work, and her life, the themes, the 'Dance of Life', 'Building Resilience', and the 'Dance of

Love' are prominent. She loves to guide others in their healing process, and provide training and mentoring. One of her passions is facilitating self love and loving, collaborative partnership.

Deborah is a Licensed Psychotherapist, EMDR Certified Therapist, and EMDRIA Approved Consultant. In her practice, she incorporates evidence based, neuro-pathway building EMDR, with mindfulness approaches and Art Therapy. Deborah Nielsen is known for her dynamic balance of compassion and fierce courage. She acts as a guide for getting obstacles out of the way, so one can be free to develop greater insight and compassion. When we are able to resonate with our core self, we are able to resonate with our true partner and to "Be in the Dance of Love."

Joni Young

Joni Young is a CEO mentor, international entrepreneur, author, speaker, philanthropist, and real estate investor. More significantly, she is a happy wife, a proud mother, and a spirit-driven servant of God. Joni is the Founder and Chairman of Joni Young Global and She Leaders United.

Joni Young Global is an international consulting firm. Joni and her team work in a customized manner with CEOs' and top leaders of high performance companies.

She Leaders United is a global organization on a mission to serve as the bridge of resources. Its purpose is to empower and form collaborations among women entrepreneurs worldwide to support the fight against breast cancer, domestic violence, and sex trade in SE Asia.

Previously, Joni served as the CEO of a $20 million international company which she built from the ground up. She took her team through the storm during the 2008 economic crash and grew the business exponentially, all while encountering breast cancer with surgeries and chemotherapy treatments.

Joni's life-long practice of servant leadership blossomed as a young immigrant from Taiwan. She launched her first cash flow business at age ten without speaking English when driven by a relentless desire to help her family through the financial struggles. Joni moved on to win many top producer awards while building her direct sales businesses. After college, she pursued a career in law as a result of a cultural belief that only doctors/lawyers/accountants/engineers are "real careers." Joni worked as a senior litigation paralegal for several years while going to law school in the evenings. When faced with the reality of her true passion in entrepreneurship, she turned to real estate. She sold 19 homes in one month and developed 600 homes in 6 years handling over $380 million in transactions. Then Joni moved on to financial services and was known as the top producer with 102% closing ratio. Simultaneously, she also became the most sought after elite sales trainer that took her around the country to conduct trainings for small groups in conference halls up to 50,000 people in auditoriums.

Although regarded as an entrepreneurial expert and warrior, Joni has a very tender and soft heart. Her life's mission has always been to serve her loved ones, to lead with global causes, and to live each day being happy and in love. She embraces in the freedom that stems from her kindred relationship with God, who ultimately is the director of her why, give, and ask.

Joni has a love story that demonstrates fate in real time and faith in motion. She shares her eventful life with her husband who is also her best friend. Together they've journeyed through the darkest of dark time and reached the highest of high point. They have traveled the world to conduct businesses and to help the poor and needy. They consciously live in a beautiful unity of falling in love with each other everyday.

Joni thrives on building business success for entrepreneurs and creating alliance among women leaders to serve global causes.

Dr. Sky Blossoms

Who thought that growing up behind the Iron Curtain, in a family of secret healers, would lead to becoming a #1 Bestselling and Award-winning Author. As a medically trained doctor and a 3rd generational healer, Dr. Sky Blossoms has worked with elite performers, celebrities, and prominent professionals at the top of their field to help them achieve emotional strength and heart opening.

Most people want a soul-mate, but what they really want is to stop holding themselves back, recapture their natural confidence, and be loved for who they are.

Dr. Sky is known as "Elite Relationship Expert" for helping clients all over the world to build passionate, meaningful, and lasting relationships. Her background in a medical field, two decades of studying psychology, neuroscience, and human behavior allow her to combine science and spirituality to achieve optimal and lasting results.

She believes that when your heart is open to Love, you become ultimately attractive, unapologetically authentic, and your life turns into an ecstatic stream of synchronicities.

Dr. Sky's passion for relationships emerged out of traumatic experience of separation from her parents at the age of 11. Her character and survival skills were forged through a series of challenges that most Americans cannot even imagine. She says that a sense of humor and lightheartedness helped her through the struggle.

In the process of her own healing and consciously opening her heart to unconditional love, Dr. Sky's unique talent was revealed. She can get to the core of the issue faster than anyone else. Clients praise her for helping them achieve more in a couple of months than 30 years of therapy.

Through intricate re-wiring of neurological pathways and belief-system alignment, she helps them permanently dissolve holdbacks and tap into their hidden potential.

The name Sky Blossoms was chosen to replace a tongue-twister birth name and to represent her commitment to live boundlessly and opening ever so fully to love.

Dr. Sky has been featured on CBS Radio, Boston Business Journal, Fox News, and ABC among others.

When Dr. Sky is not consulting, speaking, or leading retreats, she can be found dancing Argentine Tango, exploring the hidden parts of the world, sailing, hiking, or soaking in a hot spring.

Discover how to be the best ever version of yourself and genuinely attract a mate who'll treat you the way you always wanted to be treated. Be sure to check Dr. Sky's new course "Effortless Relationships Blueprint".

Christine Dunn

Christine is The Lesbian Love Guru, Transformational Love Guide, and intimacy expert specializing in working with the lesbian and queer community.

After struggling for years to make her first relationship work, she decided to learn everything she possibly could about relationships, communication, intimacy, human psychology, and most importantly - loving yourself. Christine never thought her journey to create lasting love in her own life would lead her to a dramatic career change but it did. Her quest took her around the world and finally to Tony Robbin's Namale Resort in Fiji for a Life Mastery Retreat. While attending Tony's seminar she realized there were a lot of women just like her struggling to attract their soul mate and cultivate a deeply meaningful, passionate relationship that lasts. She decided right then and there she would take all her knowledge and put it to good use helping others.

Since 2011 she's helped thousands of women find love and create extraordinary relationships through her videos, books, blog, online and live workshops, and one-on-one private coaching. She's been invited to speak on the Conscious LGBTQI Love Telesummit and Happy, Healthy Lesbian Telesummit, write for the LGBT Relationship Network and has been featured in Go Magazine, on QueerFatFemme.com, and on CardCarryingLesbian.com. Her articles have appeared on Huffington Post Online, YourTango, and HER. In 2015 she wrote "The Lesbian Intimacy Manual: 28 Days to Deeper Intimacy & Connection" with her partner Leah Love to share the principles of Conscious Love, Sacred Sexuality, Spiritual Partnerships, and Tantra with the lesbian community.

As a Transformational Love Guide, Christine provides her clients a safe, supportive, and judgment-free space to discuss their love and relationship challenges. She leads singles through a powerful process to align them with love and attract their soul mates with ease. She helps them uncover and resolve hidden challenges that have held them back from experiencing the love they truly deserve with remarkable results. For couples experiencing a relationship challenge she supports them in quickly move from despair, frustration, anger, and overwhelm into feeling empowered with the tools they need to create the best relationship of their lives!

Christine currently lives in Austin, Texas with her partner Leah Love and two beautiful daughters. They jokingly call their household a zoo because they are animal lovers with two dogs, two mini pigs, a lizard, a cat, and probably some chickens, bunnies, or ferrets (who knows what they'll adopt next!). When they're not laying in the hammock together basking in the sunshine, they're working on bringing more love into the world. Leah is a Tantra Goddess, Sacred Sexuality and Intimacy expert who helps women reclaim their sexual prowess. Together they teach intimacy and communication for couples, Tantra, erotic empowerment, sacred sexuality, and healing through touch.

Dr. Elena Estanol

Dr. Estanol is a peak performance psychologist and Intuitive Business Mentor, passionate about helping heart-centered entrepreneurs, turn their passions into profitable and transformational businesses. She has helped thousands of clients heal their bodies, step up to bigger stages, and build 6-Figure conscious businesses.

She loves to empower & mentor coaches, therapists, healers, holistic practitioners, and creatives to rise up from their challenges, conquer their fears and live life audaciously guided by love, intuition & abundance, to become transformational leaders in our world. She passionately mentors entrepreneurs to choreograph their "soul's dance" through conscious & profitable businesses, with ease, grace & a little "click of the heels."

The incredible phoenix-like transformation in her own life, through divorce, an eating disorder, foreclosure, and traumatic injuries brought her back to the power of self-love and abundance. Dr. Estanol has a Ph.D. in Counseling Psychology, a M.S. in Peak Performance & Sport Psychology, an M.F.A. in Kinesiology, Choreography and Pedagogy and a B.F.A. in teaching & dance performance. The combination of over 20 years of education, her experience and vulnerability create a deep connection that inspires her audiences & clients.

Dr. Elena guides her clients through a proven system to breakthrough internal barriers to success, reconnect with their intuition, attract ideal clients, create brilliant programs, enroll clients easily and create lasting change in the world, while making money and having fun!

Dr. Elena loves to share her wisdom through speaking, workshops, masterminds and group coaching programs. She thrives on witnessing the transformation evident through mastermind groups in elevating spirit, impact & income.

She has founded 3 different businesses:
- Luminescent Life LLC (An Intuitive Prosperity & Business Coaching Practice focused on helping heart-based entrepreneurs create 6-Figure conscious businesses, while creating the life of their dreams & elevating their spirit.)
- Phoenix Rising LLC- a real-estate and property management company) and
- Synapse Counseling LLC (An integrative wellness & coaching practice focused on treating eating disorders, ADHD, nutrition, body image and empowerment coaching.)

Her previous publications include:
- "Dance Psychology for Artistic & Performance Excellence". (co-authored with Dr. Jim Taylor)
- "The Relationship between Risk and resilience factors for eating disorders in Dancers"

Dr. Estanol is still dancing and performing as an aerial dancer, and loves to read, write, hike and do yoga. She lives in Fort Collins, CO, surrounded by loving friends, an incredible staff, and her fabulous husband and life partner, with whom she works, plays, and co-creates a fun, happy and abundant life. He is an Integrative Nutrition & Wellness Coach, and they share their home with their two (very spoiled) kitties: Romeo & Othello.

IMPORTANT
We have powerful, life changing GIFTS for you.

Each author has created a gift or two for you to help you get more shifts. Most of these are required for the best breakthroughs as you read each chapter. These include audios, videos, and templates. Go now and get your conscious love bonus gifts here:

http://blisslifepress.com/conscious-love/bonuses/

This is a BlissLife Press
"Profitable Philanthropy" Book
Become A Conscious Book Ambassador
For Love
Ask Us How

We are proud to partner with a philanthropy for this book project. Our mission with this book is to support funds solving Domestic Violence. From education, to women's shelters, all funds raised and two thirds of the proceeds from the sale of this book will go to help change loving relationships by empowering women to know their value and have resources to turn to in times of need.

Please go to http://blisslifepress.com/ambassador/ or email support@blisslifepress.com to receive more information on the philanthropy for this particular book. Email and say: "I want to be an Ambassador for Love"! We will be doing a fundraiser for this charity online, and would love for you to help us spread the word, so we can make a big difference for a multitude of people.

Become a Conscious Book Ambassador... ask us how.

A "Profitable Philanthropy Book" is a program where we pair each author's book to a philanthropy that is relevant to the author's topic, and passions and create a synergistic relationship with multiple benefits.

We do an actual fundraiser for the cause, which, along with the bestseller campaign, multiplies the reach and interest through the media we line up for the book launch. This raises funds and awareness about the cause as well as a tribe and clients for the author's book, business and message.

Thank you for helping us make a profound difference through this program. We LOVE win-win-win experiences! Another way 'Books Save Lives'!

Our Passions:
We plant hundreds of trees for each book we publish. We LOVE trees!
We fund a woman's business for each book. We LOVE entrepreneurs!
We give to creativity and art funds. We LOVE self expression and beauty!
We give one online course for each purchased. We LOVE transformation!

BlissLife Press

Purpose - Philanthropy - Profits - Planet - Peace - Prosperity - Partnership

BlissLife Press

BlissLife Press is an award winning publishing house leading an emerging global 'Conscious Business' movement to transform lives through adding "Profitable Philanthropy" and conscious marketing to our authors books and business.

If you are a professional speaker, a coach, a healer, or a web and marketing expert - You need a book! Your unique life story combined with your system for helping clients in a published book will be your most powerful client attraction, marketing and money making tool. We bring in world class expert trainers, and we help with marketing, media, publishing, bestseller campaigns and launch you as a global leader.

We are entrepreneurs, marketers, business builders and bestselling authors, with over 30 years experience. We know, as an expert in your field, you have a calling within your heart that says help more people, make a difference to the planet, make a bigger impact, give and make more money. You want to start and grow a movement. You know you were meant for greater things. Now is the time to write your book and integrate profitable philanthropy so you can multiply your time, money and efforts.

How can writing a conscious business book help you grow your business? Your business can benefit massively from a book positioning you as a leading expert.

7 Profitable Reasons to Write a Book for Your Business
1. Be known! Get Media
2. Open doors!
3. Attract more clients!
4. Establish your expert status!
5. Higher Fees!
6. Be seen as a Leader!
7. Make a Bigger Impact!

Don't pour your heart and soul into a book, only to be disappointed with a few sales and dollars that most authors I meet experience. Do what you were designed to do, and leave the marketing, media, and list building to us. We launch you and show you how to use your book's success to grow your business and make a difference. Talk to us.

Please visit http://blisslifepress.com/ to receive - as our gift - Video Training: "How to Make an extra $100,000 in the Next 90 Days using something we call Profitable Philanthropy" & "How to Write a Book - You Love - in 30 Days" Step by Step Blueprint Chart

BlissLife Press
- Profitable Philanthropy Book Launches - Marketing, Publishing, Media, Launch
- Conscious Business Client Magnet Book
- Conscious Collaborations Co-Authored Books - (12 Authors max) a Profitable Philanthropy Project

BlissLife Press
Purpose - Philanthropy - Profits - Planet - Peace - Prosperity - Partnership

Proof

Made in the USA
Charleston, SC
17 July 2016